PARADISE LOST

Michael James Elves

Grosvenor House
Publishing Limited

This book is published by
Grosvenor House Publishing Ltd
Link House
140 The Broadway, Tolworth, Surrey, KT6 7HT.
www.grosvenorhousepublishing.co.uk

A CIP record for this book
is available from the British Library

ISBN 978-1-80381-467-4
eBook ISBN 978-1-80381-468-1

CONTENTS

INTRODUCTION

On the island of Zakynthos, in the Greek Islands, a man was born. This man was to become an important figure to the future of the loggerhead turtles (*Caretta caretta*), and the wildlife that lives on the island, including the wild flowers and other plantation that are native to this island.

There were to be great changes on the island that would leave the wildlife that lives here to become endangered. This enemy was to become known as tourism. The man, Yannis Vardakastanis, realised this and was determined to do something about it.

That is exactly what he did. He started a turtle sanctuary in Vasilikos to try to preserve the wildlife, especially the loggerhead sea turtles that nest on the island's beaches.

Friends, officials, and also family for a while turned against him but this became a passion and Yannis' thoughts were for the preservation of his beloved island and to try to protect the wildlife from certain decline, hopefully for a bit longer.

Yannis knows full well that one day all will be lost and this wonderful island will be guilty of turning its back on what makes this island of Zakynthos so special!

This book is not just about Yannis Vardakastanis – and he would not want it to be – but the preservation of this island. All the wildlife that enjoys the beauty of this very special island could be vanishing at a very fast rate! It is our duty to stand behind this amazing man and help in his work to keep this island that we all enjoy healthy for all things that live here. Let's not lose it for good!

This land of ours is a paradise, and with your help we can continue to keep it that way, but we must act now or it will just become a PARADISE LOST!

THE AUTHOR MICHAEL JAMES ELVES

MICHAEL JAMES ELVES
THE AUTHOR

Born in 1949 in Dagenham on the outskirts of London, I went to a secondary modern school called Goresbrooke. Leaving school when I was 15, I started my working life in 1964 as a trainee chef for Mecca restaurants where I worked in Cheapside, London Wall, and Threadneedle Street. I then decided to join a band as a drummer and was in several bands for many years and also jammed with Eric Clapton. I met my wife-to-be when she was just 14 and have been with her now for over 50 years. I still play the drums to this day.

I became an oil painter when I was 23 and have since had many exhibitions. My writing started about 30 years ago when I wrote my very first story for my grandson, Christian. Children's stories were my favourite then and I went on to write many more, well over 100.

I then got my first children's book published, *Bedtime Tales of Europe*, which can be found on Amazon.

In time, I wanted to try writing stories for adults. Most of my stories are short as I do not like to drag a story out as I feel many people can become bored with it if it is dragged out too long. Then I wanted to try to write a play, which I did, and although never used, I got satisfying comments from the people I had sent it to. This in turn led me to write a film script, which I am hoping to have luck with in the near future.

I am now at the young age of 72 and I live on the island of Zakynthos, Greece. This is where the idea came from for *Paradise Lost*. Talking to Yannis Vardakastanis one day, he asked me if I would write a book on the turtle sanctuary that he runs and about the man himself who is trying desperately to preserve the loggerhead turtles that nest on Zakynthos' beaches, and the wildlife that lives on this lovely island. I could not refuse him as I have so much respect for what he is desperately trying to do for the preservation of his island. I hope once you have read this book you will see the importance of preserving not just this island, but our beautiful planet.

MAUREEN ELIZABETH ELVES
PHOTOGRAPHER

I would like to thank Maureen for taking most of the photographs in this book. When I asked if she would agree to taking on the task, she was happy to oblige.

We went out in all the seasons of the year so that we could get the shots that I was looking for, mostly on the motorbike, going through the mountains, looking for the right shot. Several photos were taken of flowers that grow on this island of Zakynthos. Birds, frogs, etc., were captured to hopefully describe the amazing wildlife that lives here. We could not use all the photographs that Maureen took, although it would have been nice, but it would be very easy to turn the book into a photo album. We hope that the ones we have entered in the book will be more than enough to give you an idea on how much beauty is on this island. Yannis Vardakastanis knows very well how much beauty there is on this island, but he also knows if things do not change for the better, then this paradise will certainly be lost and lost forever.

Thank you, Maureen, for your help in making this book possible. Your devoted husband, Mike.

ONE MAN'S DREAM

The Greek Islands have always fascinated a lot of people. They have journeyed from all over the world to holiday on the islands. The islands bring immeasurable pleasure to all those that visit, whether it is the Aegean or the Ionian Islands, each one with its own identity.

No less can be said for Zakynthos, one of the islands in the Ionian. This island can boast of being one of the most important for its turtles, which nest every year on its many beaches. The turtle, known as the loggerhead, or better known locally as *Caretta caretta*, are in decline. Zakynthos has, through the years, become popular with a wealth of tourists, which in turn could endanger the survival of these now rare turtles. Indeed, other wildlife is confronted with this problem as well and is also struggling to hold its ground.

This is a story about one man's dream.

He was born on the island in 1964, and has lived here all his life. The man's name is Yannis Vardakastanis. He was a boy like any other, playing in the fields that surrounded his parents' house that supported the family with produce that his mother and father grew, as well as the livestock, which supplied them with the meat and dairy products that they needed.

Yannis helped his parents, often with the help of his four brothers, one of which was his twin. His three sisters did no less in the task of helping to support the family. These were happy days, though, and life was a simple and peaceful existence.

Yannis' first awareness of the wildlife that surrounded him was on one of the local beaches, Gerakas. His first venture there was when he was at the young age of six years old. He was astonished to see so much wildlife – crabs, turtles, birds of all different species. Wild flowers and shrubbery were in abundance growing inland. Even at this young age, Yannis realised what a rich and fertile paradise this land that he lived in was, and it was at this moment he became interested in the preservation of all the wildlife that lived on this wonderful island of his.

His parents' house was a humble two-bedroomed house. In one of these bedrooms slept all of the children, eight of them in all. The house still stands to this day, reminding him of his childhood days.

Yannis' first day at school was without the luxury of shoes. This continued until he was eight years old, a luxury that maybe was long awaited.

The school in Vasilikos that Yannis attended was small and only a short walk from Gerakas where he lived. Indeed, Gerakas was his place of birth, from which he never left. During his school days, he also attended school in Athens where he spent the last five years of his school life.

At the age of 17, Yannis decided to join the navy, which took him around most of the world. He enjoyed countries like India and Australia. This he did for a further five years. Travelling made him always think of his beloved Zakynthos, and his home. After leaving the navy, he decided to open a beach bar on Gerakas beach. The year was 1987. This bar continued to run until 1991, with a chain of sunbeds positioned near the bar.

Yannis decided to finish with the bar and sunbed business on the beach and pulled the bar down. This did not go down too well with one of his brothers, who helped Yannis run the business. Yannis' passion for the wildlife, which depended on the beach, overtook the lust for money and the brothers fell out. This upset Yannis, but he realised that his business was helping to destroy wildlife and that would not be acceptable. This was his home as well and he wanted it to stay in the healthy state that he has always known it.

In 1991, Yannis decided to visit England. He stayed in Dorset and then Putney in London. He was 26 years old now and extended his stay in England for a further 10 years. Within those years, he started a holiday business, which helped him learn the English language, which proved to be very useful in the future. In 1993, Yannis decided to build a sanctuary for the turtles and other wildlife as part of his passion. This was built in wood and was of a basic style. The plan, however, was to rebuild it in stone as to make it lifelong.

It was the turtles and the love of them that extended his passion, and also for the other wildlife that fought for their daily survival. Yannis travelled regularly from England to Zakynthos to build the sanctuary with his own hands. This was the start of one man's dream, which will have no ending.

TOURISM

Tourism started in the early '80s, and more sunbeds and bars were thrust onto the beaches. This in turn started the demise of the nesting spots for the loggerhead turtles, and started to cause problems for the wildlife.

The lights on the bars at night became an enemy for the turtle eggs that had been laid in the sand. As once the eggs hatched, the young turtles, who rely on the moon's light to guide them to the water's edge, would become confused. The lights of the bars would sometimes make the turtles go the opposite way from the sea, which would be a deadly mistake for the hatchlings. They would only too often get run over by the cars on the road in front of the bars. Some would just get lost and dehydrate on the beach, or be too exhausted to go further. For them, death was imminent.

Sunbeds played their part also, as they would also become an obstacle that the hatchlings could not get over. Tourists swamped the beaches, with children digging holes in the sand, and building sandcastles. Although this is a normal part of holiday enjoyment, tourists were unaware that they were contributing to the demise of these wonderful creatures that have outlived the dinosaurs.

Yannis' concerns were growing rapidly. The turtles were finding less and less beach to nest on. The island's tourism was growing fast! Of course, there was money to be made from this now growing industry. This benefitted the islanders by giving them a better financial life. Hotels and self-catering studios were being created throughout the island. The turtles themselves became famous to the tourists that visited, and soft toys, t-shirts and even china models of turtles were sold in the tourist shops that were popping up all over the island. Even boat trips were, and are still, offered to the excited tourist, so that they could see the turtles swimming in the bays, the Bay of Laganas and Kalamaki being the most popular.

The island's wealth was continuing to grow. This made Yannis' concerns even greater than before. The fear of losing even more turtles, and indeed other important wildlife to the tourist industry, was now becoming somewhat of a nightmare!

It was not just the tourists that were causing problems, but in some cases the native people of Zakynthos as well!

Casting rubbish into the sea was, and still is, a big problem. Things such as fishing lines, plastic bottles, discarded fish netting and of course the deadly plastic bag, which are cast from the boats. All these things and much more play their part in the destruction of these wonderful turtles. Plastic bags which float in the sea are mistaken by the turtles for jellyfish, which is part of the turtles' diet. The bags are eaten, which then cannot be digested. This will cause a terrible prolonged death. This is a most horrific way to die, something not one of us could possibly imagine. Can you imagine stuffing a plastic bag down your throat and waiting for that horrific, very slow end to come?

Fishing lines can be responsible for horrific injuries. They can get entangled around the turtles' fins, cutting deep into them. This will cause them a great deal of stress and make swimming properly impossible. Sometimes the turtle will be totally exhausted, which in turn will terminate the creature's life.

All these things can be easily avoided by not discarding rubbish into the sea. Rubbish on the beaches can be removed and put into rubbish bins. This very small chore can save a turtle's life. My wife and I walk the beaches of Kalamaki and Laganas regularly, especially in the winter months. We pick up rubbish as we go, sometimes entering the sea to remove plastic bags and bottles that have washed up with the tide. This small chore can also be effective in the summer months, just by removing any rubbish that could be floating in the sea and, of course, taking any rubbish that you have accumulated whilst on the beach with you when leaving. It is a small task, but if you think like my wife and indeed myself, hopefully you will get the same satisfaction as we do, knowing that this could save a turtle's life. Some of the rubbish is discarded by fishing boats, maybe by accident, sometimes intentional, and if that is the case, a lot of the rubbish could be prevented. They really need to play their part as well. It is such a small thing to do, but pays a big reward!

Kalamaki and Laganas are part of the National Marine Park. They do their part every year by monitoring the nests as they arrive, but there is still room for improvement. Cleaning the beaches more often would help considerably. Having more rubbish bins distributed along the beach would be a great advantage. It's an ongoing task, as it is unfortunately regular for plastic bags, bottles, etc. to constantly turn up on the beach. Sometimes oil cans show their unwanted heads, which leaves stains on the sand from the oil. This would be a problem also for other life in the sea and can cause drastic effects for the future of the sea life.

I think that National Marine Life could do so much better. In the summer I watch them walk up and down the beach holding their all-important monitoring boards. I have no doubt that they are checking the nests where the turtles have been busily laying their eggs. They make sure that all sunbeds and parasols are nearer to the water's edge. This being a credit to them all. The only thing that worries me is the fact that they do not know where all the nests are! Surely if the beach is being monitored, it would be around the clock, making sure that they know exactly where these nests are! They are taught to recognise a fresh turtle's nest, so I don't really understand this problem. I suppose if they don't monitor 24 hours a day there is certainly a very good chance of missing some nests. Please don't think I'm knocking the employees of the National Marine Park, but there is always room for improvement. I have noticed that also some of the sunbeds creep dangerously near to the nests, which are visible by wooden frames that surround them. This must be dealt with, or the nests could be in danger of being destroyed.

Yannis' main energy centres on the beach of Gerakas. This is where he had his bar, boat, and sunbed business. As I have mentioned earlier, this caused a certain amount of trouble when he decided to move his bar further inland. The boat and sunbed side of things he discontinued. Yannis tried to convince others to do the same, which apparently did not go down too well! He and two of his brothers were beaten up for their efforts, leaving Yannis with a number of broken ribs and abrasions. One man also tried to express his opinion by attempting to shoot Yannis with a shotgun. Luckily, Yannis was too near the man and managed to avert this insane act!

After a long struggle, he managed to ensure there were fewer sunbeds and boats on Gerakas beach.

At one time, there were as many as 180 parasols, 32 pedalos, and about 20 canoes, plus two bars on the beach. You can imagine the congestion was a very dangerous enemy to the wildlife, affecting turtles especially.

THE SIMPLE DAYS

Going back some years, to before Yannis was born, indeed back almost 200 years, the area of Vasilikos was mostly farmland and his family and ancestors all worked the land. They crops such as grapes, olives, vegetables, and of course rearing the livestock. Life was very hard, and his ancestors especially had to toil the land with just hand tools and maybe the odd horse. A long and very tiring task that took them from early morning to late into the evening. Every day the same, come wind, sun, or rain. The land was not owned by his family, and they were paid very poorly. Although I would have thought that they were allowed some of the produce that had been grown.

The water that they drank and washed in came from a well. This well is still visible today. It makes you wonder how lucky we are today. Just imagine having to draw water from a well every time it was needed. Rain or shine, this chore had to be done regardless and, of course, hoping that the crops that were planted would be enough to sustain everyone. It must have been a never-ending worry. Survival must have been always in a fine balance. The well was still used when Yannis was a boy, so things really did not change too much until his teen years.

The wildlife was in abundance though, and there were as many as 426 species of birds that were either native to the island or would migrate there every year. A vast difference from the amount today. I am a keen birdwatcher myself, and I have noticed the difference in the number of birds since I first came to the island as a tourist some 26 years ago. I am very happy to be living on the island now, but, like Yannis, very concerned about the future of the wildlife, fauna and flora that at the moment exists on this lovely island.

Before Zakynthos had an airport, the land was an abundance of marshland. Imagine how much life that land could sustain.

Flamingos in their thousands lived on the marshes. There were many herons, storks, and egrets. Birds of prey were more common, especially the golden eagle – which would prey on flamingos – buzzards, kite falcons (such as the peregrine and Eleonora's falcon) all benefitted from the marsh. Smaller birds like the greenfinch, great tits, yellowhammer, sparrows and many warblers would feed from the marsh, not forgetting the insects, such as beetles, mayfly, and, of course, the amazing dragonfly and butterflies. It was a haven for wildlife. Wild flowers grew in their thousands, also. It must have been a tremendously exciting place.

Today there are much bigger birds landing there: we call them planes. Flamingos were never to be seen there again. There are a few herons, mostly seen on the salt lakes of Alykes. Possibly a solitary heron will be seen flying across the bay of Kalamaki and Laganas. Storks are very rare, but I have seen the odd one. The island has reintroduced the golden eagle, but only a few pairs. I fully understand that the island's tourism is important to its financial growth, but what a shame that the wildlife has to pay so dearly.

Before Yannis was born, the island suffered, like so many countries in Europe, the Second World War.

The area of Vasilikos was now in the war, accommodating Germans and Italians. There were many. There were big guns placed on the hills overlooking the local people's houses, including Yannis' parents, the Italians apparently staying on the beach of Gerakas. This must have been an extremely worrying time for Yannis' parents, Panaqiotis and Georgina, wondering what was going to become of them. Worrying times indeed! It's hard to imagine that these peaceful farming folk were subjected to those aliens that had taken control of their small island. I don't know if they played a part in supporting these unwanted guests by denying themselves of the little food that was so scarce in these troubled times. It was certain, however, that the Germans and the Italians sometimes killed turtles and dug up the eggs to enhance their diet.

This would have been possibly catastrophic for the survival of the turtle and certainly played a big part in their demise. Turtles live for about 80 years; they lay their eggs every year from May to September and it takes six to eight weeks for their incubation period to be completed, some 100 or more eggs in each nest. So the loss was certainly many.

The turtles' struggle for survival starts as soon as they are laid. Nature itself can be a big danger to the eggs' survival, storms for one can be devastating, as the nests get submerged in water which will in turn drown the young turtles before they are even hatched! I think it was the year 2012 that the island suffered the loss of no less than 40 percent of its turtle eggs this way.

Of course, other enemies exist to the young turtles once they have hatched. The beach itself can be a menacing place also, with the help of parasols, sunbeds, and tourists digging holes in the sand and building castles. Of course, it's very understandable that families, especially with young children, want to play with the sand. We all have participated in this very enjoyable pastime, it's part of being on holiday and having fun and who wants to destroy this masterpiece that you have lovingly built? This, though, is something that you must do at the end of the day – unfilled holes and intact castles could become a big hazard to the new hatchlings. If holes and castles are left, then they may become the young turtles' killer, as falling into a hole could make it difficult for the hatchling to climb out again! The sandcastles become lethal obstacles; it could confuse the turtle. The young turtles' objective is to head straight for the sea, so it is vital that these creatures have no objects to conquer, just by leaving the beach in a tidy state will help them reach their destination. It seems only fair that we give these animals a better chance of survival. Plastic bottles, plastic bags, glass bottles, discarded beach toys such as buckets and spades, can play a devastating role in their surviving numbers. Only one or two hatchlings from a thousand eggs will survive. They have many enemies that are natural enemies, such as seagulls and crabs, that lay in wait as they take their first perilous journey to the water's edge. Then there are the dangers once they enter the unknowable sea. Their young lives are almost certain to be in constant danger. The lucky survivors will not return to that beach of their birth for another two decades when they will lay their own eggs.

The male species, however, will never return, as they spend the rest of their long lives in the sea. The amount of nests in 2013, I believe, was around the figure of 1500. In 2014, there were less than 1000. So it is not too hard to imagine that, if the nests continue to be destroyed, in about 50 years these magnificent loggerhead turtles could cease to exist on the island of Zakynthos! If a nesting turtle is injured whilst making the incredibly long journey back to her birthplace and dies through the injury, it would not be just the turtle that is lost, but all of her eggs as well. Okay, we now know that only one or two young turtles survive out of a thousand, but who can be sure that the dying turtles eggs could all be successful in surviving, and if that was the case, they would be the only lucky survivors out of around 50 to 100,000. I can fully understand Yannis' concerns for the protection of these amazing creatures.

For someone to be so passionate about the wildlife on this island of Zakynthos deserves total recognition indeed!

When Yannis started to build the sanctuary in 1993, he at first built it for Archelon to run, but a while later Yannis began to run it himself. I don't know the reason he decided to do that, but he has certainly been successful. The sanctuary is supported by the sea life and Earth, Sea & Sky organisations, also donations from visitors abroad are well received.

Yannis has spent years getting the sanctuary to where it is today. This man never stops, he is very much a man on a mission. He works all year round striving further forward. The sanctuary is very different now, built in stone with an outbuilding that accommodates four very large tanks made of glass. The glass is incredibly strong – it as to be as they hold thousands of litres of water. The water must be pumped twenty-four hours a day to stop it from stagnating. This was also built by Yannis and some of the volunteers that come over to the island every year, normally from the Earth, Sea & Sky organisation. On occasion, some independent volunteers also help out.

The volunteers also help explain to the visitors, for example, why the turtles are a threatened species and help them learn how to reduce the threat by abiding to simple rules.

The visitors are sometimes puzzled about the lack of turtles in the sanctuary, but they must realise that this is a good thing. If there are no turtles in the sanctuary, then there have not been any found injured. Of course, I can understand their disappointment; everyone would like to come face to face with one of these wonderful creatures, but imagine the disappointment of the turtle if he was there.

Although the sanctuary is mainly for those turtles that do get injured, it is also for all the wildlife on the island that suffer injury. Yannis would not turn any distressed animal away from the safe walls of the sanctuary.

The sanctuary is really worth a visit. Yannis Vardakastanis' tireless efforts make the sanctuary and indeed the whole of the Gerakas area worth a visit. His bar is within yards of the sanctuary. This can be enjoyed by the visitors also, as they can snack and enjoy a cool drink after seeing the sanctuary, but you must realise that the sanctuary is not a gimmick for his bar. Yannis is more than happy to explain his concerns for the turtles and for the rest of the wildlife that live on the island. There are, however, some doubting people out there that think the sanctuary is just a money-spinner for his bar. What I would say to them is if they had done a fraction of what this remarkable man has achieved? They would probably be the first to tell everyone!

Yannis is an extraordinary man; there is no blowing his own trumpet, he prefers to be left to do the work that he is so passionate about. Don't talk to him about politics, he is not interested!

At Gerakas beach, there is a pathway on top of the cliff just before the steps that lead to the beach. It is very much worth a walk along it. There you can see wildlife such as birds, warblers, and robins that migrate to the island every year. This was something that I did not realise: as a native to England, I know that robins are a full-time resident there, and I did not realise that they were a migrating bird in other countries, so I was a bit surprised by that.

There is an abundance of different butterflies as well, some small like the little blue, then there is the most magnificent swallowtails. There is one butterfly – I think from the swallowtail family – that when you see it, it looks upside down! This, however, is a defence for the butterfly, it has black or brown stripes on a white background and the butterfly, I can assure you, is certainly the right way up! The place itself will tell you why Yannis loves the area so much. I find the colonies of ants that live there fascinating. They are busily running up and down the cliff pathway in single file. I find it amazing what these creatures can carry – I think ten times their own weight – and they never give up when they are carrying or dragging a carcass of some demised beetle or grasshopper. I have seen the odd lizard scurry away as one of the larger breed of ant sank its pincers into its nose! I admire these creatures, and give them the respect that they fully deserve, so please be careful when walking, make sure that you are not treading on them. After all their efforts, they don't deserve a size nine boot wiping them out.

Dafni beach is another beach that the turtles nest on. The surrounding area, with its mountainous ranges and valleys, is breathtaking. This beach is also protected strictly by law. Dafni beach is between Kalamaki and Gerakas, but it is unfortunate that there are tavernas along the beach, and I am a bit surprised that the local authorities tolerate it. If it is strictly protected, then surely that's exactly what should happen. It is protected by the Marine Park organisation and has its wardens on the beach, but unfortunately there seems to be a lapse of concern for this particular beach. The beach is still very important for the turtles to lay their eggs. Maybe the concerns will grow as there become fewer and fewer nests.

The area of Dafni has some nice surprises though. There are two very narrow roads leading to Dafni beach, and I am surprised that anybody can reach the beach area, unless they possess a four-wheel drive truck or a scrambling bike. The roads are very rugged and mostly made of a very lumpy layer of concrete or mud. The mud gets washed away by the rains, making it almost impossible to drive or ride! There certainly is a tremendous amount of loose stone, and the gullies that are made by the falling rains can be very deep. Some parts of the roads are built looking as if they have subsided, so they are very difficult to pass. I really don't know how some of the tourists make it down there at all. I have the greatest amount of sympathy for the rental cars and bikes that take this perilous journey down to the beach. It certainly would be an experience. Having said all that, I think the hills and valleys are superb. If like me you like a walk, this would be an excellent place for it. Make sure you have the correct footwear on though, as you will definitely need it.

The wildlife around this area is brilliant, it has something for everybody. The bird life is alive with different species; I can almost guarantee you will see a buzzard or a kite. If you are very lucky, a golden eagle might make an appearance. Peregrine, or the Eleonora's falcon also can be spotted.

The Eleonora's falcon is my favourite. The bird was named after a medieval princess, who put a protection order on Sardinia's birds of prey. The bird has a dark phase and a light phase. It's principally a migratory bird, but some do remain in the eastern Mediterranean region. They are very fast and agile, and they catch their prey in flight, whether it be a small bird or an insect. The Eleonora's falcon often hunts in flocks late in the evening. The bird is in between a peregrine and a hobby in size, and can be recognised by its long wings.

The smaller birds are worth a mention too, and black redstart, great tits, and warblers are frequently seen as well as other species of small birds. The sparrow has my respect. It is a very hardy bird, and seems to be able to survive all types of weather. The nightingale can also be heard singing its most beautiful song, although this would not be a bird that can be seen often, as it is not a common bird for Zakynthos, but you could be lucky.

Warblers are also a favourite of mine. The Sardinian warbler for one, with its black hood and white breast. The female lacks the black hood, but still has a white breast. The male, though, is definitely the easiest to spot, and of course we cannot forget the black redstart with its brick-red tail and grey back with a splash of white and black face. The female would have the brick-red tail, but would be grey without the black colouration on its face, still a lovely bird though.

There is another beach near to Dafni, but this beach is closed off to the public. The turtles do nest there and are monitored. I don't know how big or small the area of this beach is, and I have no idea why it is closed to the public. Maybe the beach *is* too small for turtles and tourists together; I shall try and find out and maybe I will be able to explain why later in the book. This will certainly be good for the turtles though. The beach is called Sekania, and you can see the whereabouts of Sekania on the Zakynthos map.

Looking over the bay of Kalamaki from Dafni, you will see a small island. This island is called Pelouzo, and if your luck is in you will see some seals that rest and breed around the area. These seals are called monk seals. I had never seen one until this year, 2015, when my wife, Maureen, and I spotted three in the bay. I have been assured that they are a regular sight, so it is possible that you might have some luck and see these delightful animals.

Pelouzo has an abundance of flora and fauna, which covers the island like a green blanket. I have no doubt that this lovely little island that sits peacefully in the Kalamaki bay also supports a multitude of wildlife that is also worthy of preservation. Going back to the Dafni area, there, close by, is an old abandoned landfill.

This concerns Yannis a great deal as the toxins from this landfill can be carried into the sea when it starts to rain. This can have a drastic effect on the life that live in the sea. I recently checked it out, and I must agree with Yannis. This issue must be looked into, and a solution reached, that prevents it seeping into the crystal-clear waters of the bay before it can do massive damage to marine life. Another problem that worries Yannis is the continuous surge of stray dogs. They are only too common on the beaches, Kalamaki and Laganas especially, though most beaches have their strays wondering up and down. Most of the dogs are friendly, and it's a complete shame that these dogs are either discarded by their owners, or they are born in the wild. Some do not survive as they might stray into the roads and get knocked over and killed. Other dogs suffer a more prolonged death, as some people see fit to poison these poor animals. These abandoned dogs, though, do dig up turtle eggs that have been buried in the sands, sometimes by sniffing them out, then devouring them. This is a great shame, as the turtles' plight for life is made even more desperate, and their fight for life is lost before it begins.

These dogs though must be kept off the beaches. If the owners of these dogs were not so cold-minded, and if they don't want the dog, then give it to someone that is willing to take it in, not just dump it. Now it's someone else's problem!

There are a few people on the island that help the dogs. Mainly they are British, and they will feed them and try to find homes for them, so well done to those people. This, though, is a continuous battle, and it must be very frustrating for them. I think there must be more that the island can do to solve this problem. I have seen so many strays since I have lived on the island, and I feel very sorry for these poor animals that do not deserve this cruel existence. I think that local government could do a lot more than they do; after all, if these strays do affect the population of turtles, then it is going to affect the island itself. As I have constantly said, turtles are one of the sources that this island needs to sustain its financial growth! When all the turtles are no more, it's no good thinking it does not matter, and it will not happen in my lifetime! It will happen in someone's lifetime, and of course by then it will be too late!

Imagine the effect, to have no turtles there will be no point in tourists going on boat trips. What are they going to see? You could put a plastic blow up turtle in the water, but I don't think that will fool anyone.

This in turn will put people out of work. This goes for any business that relies on the turtle for a living. The island of Zakynthos is known worldwide for its turtles and could possibly have the effect on tourism that this island cannot afford. It is very understandable why Yannis Vardakastanis is so concerned. This is why Yannis will never give up on what he is trying to achieve. I think that the island of Zakynthos should stand very much behind this amazing man, and help any way they can to prevent the island's certain economic demise in the very real future! This can be done so easily; it's not politics, it's a simple case of whether you want to keep the island as a paradise or not! The only way is to live in harmony, support your wildlife, and live side by side with it. This will help the future of the island for generations to come.

A TURTLE'S LIFE

I am going to try and attempt to imagine that I am a turtle, and write this story from the time it is an egg, to the time that it is an adult. You may think that I am completely mad, but I wonder what it would be like to be a turtle, and see everything that these creatures have to encounter throughout their lives. Being in the mind of a turtle is going to be difficult, but here goes anyway.

What on earth is going on! What is all this blackness that I seem to be engulfed in? I cannot seem to remember any of this! I have suddenly become aware of the tomb that surrounds me. It is very soft, but I cannot escape from this very strange prison, although I have this feeling of complete tranquillity. The warmth that surrounds me is a great comfort, but I have no idea where I am or what I am! I feel as though there are some other things surrounding me that feel very similar to myself, but what are they? I have been trapped in this soft weird thing for what seems to be ages now, and this strange object seems to be getting much tighter, and I am having trouble moving. I can feel a lot of movement around me, it is though everything is struggling the same as myself. I wonder if these things are the same things as me, and like myself, are becoming desperate to free themselves from this prison. I think it is time for me to break out of this, I feel as though I am suffocating, but also something incredibly strong wants to pull me away from this dark tomb.

At last, I am starting to break away from this strange object. I can see it starting to split, one last effort and I think that I will be free.

Yes! I have done it. The movement that surrounds me is amazingly rapid, everything is scrambling upwards. I can see something that is much lighter, and I can see strange shapes heading towards it! I must follow, it could be freedom away from this awful darkness. Scrambling upwards is very difficult, the strange substance that is beneath me seems to give way under my movements. I am slipping down again. I must take hold of something that is more solid, otherwise I shall never be free. At last there is something down here that feels more solid, if I can just pull myself above it, I might have a chance. This is exhausting, but I am managing to get nearer the top of this abyss.

At last! I never thought I would make it. I must rest a while, get my strength back. I still don't know what we all are, but we all look the same! Some are still trying to get out of this huge hole that I am looking down on. They are tumbling down on each other, and some seem to have stopped moving altogether. There is a light ahead; it seems to be drawing me and the others towards it. There is a strange liquid that I can see moving; I don't know why, but I know I must head for it. There are some much larger creatures that I can see, some are floating in mid-air! They are very big and a very light colour, and what on earth's that? It's like armour on legs, with massive claw-like things attached. It's hard work trying to push forward on this ground that moves.

What on earth is that screaming? It's coming from the large creatures that float on air. They are diving down and grabbing some of us in their mouths! Oh no, they are killing us! I must get out of here before I am killed as well. What have we done to deserve this! The armour-on-legs are grabbing us now! One of us is trapped in its claws, and is struggling to break free. It's not going to happen, the things with claws are far too strong. I'm so frightened, I must make it to the strange liquid before I, too, become a victim. I'm nearing the strange liquid now, I feel exhausted, but I must carry on, after the near miss I have just had with some of those giant claws. I just want to get into the liquid, and hopefully be safe.

It's very strange, the liquid seems to help my body to move more easily. I will try to get even deeper as I feel that I will be much safer from those evil monsters that are lurking above. I can see some objects below me, I think I will be safe there, and maybe rest a while.

I have made it! These objects are very hard and strong, I will be safe enough here while I get some rest. I wonder how many of us made it. Some of us did not, that's for sure. What an awful painful end they must have had. I can only count my blessings that I did not experience the same fate. This looks so peaceful in this liquid that I don't understand, and yet it feels as though I belong here. The feeling of contentment is overwhelming, better than the nightmare that me and so many others have just been through. There are other creatures that move around down here without any effort, but they are not bothering me at all. They seem to know what I am, I wish I did! My breathing is calming down now, and I am starting to feel more relaxed. I shall make a move soon, as I want to have a look around this strange but peaceful surround. The more I move the more I seem to want to. It's as though something is pulling me forward like a magnet.

I see some others like myself heading in the same direction; I have no doubt they are having the same feeling. I will follow for a while, but something is telling me to keep going on my own. There are some larger creatures ahead; I'm not sure I like this, but I must continue. I shall go a little deeper avoiding these strange giants. The others are all swimming together and are heading straight towards these large creatures. The large creatures have turned and noticed the rest of us. They are swimming rapidly towards us. It's happening again! The large creatures have started to attack, and are swallowing us whole! I must stay where I am, they may not notice me hidden in this long weed.

It's been a long time now, surely the giant creatures have gone. I will have to have a look; I cannot stay here much longer. I feel this strong invisible force still pulling me forward. I wish I knew what it was, though, that has this power over me.

It's been months now, and I have grown much larger. I have spoken to creatures of my own kind. They tell me that I am a turtle, a funny name, but at least I know what I am now. I am enjoying every moment gliding through this liquid that is called water. It's very clear and I can see all the other life that lives in this water. Life is not always pleasant, though, as there are some terrifying predators that I must try and avoid, which can be a little scary, as I don't wish to become someone's lunch!

Years have gone by, and I am very large now. I have also met a friend, the same species as myself. We enjoy swimming around together, discovering new exciting places. I wish that I could stay with him, but I have this urge to swim back to where I came from all those years ago. I have no idea why; all I know is that I must.

This journey is certainly exhausting, but I must continue. There is something strange about me that I don't understand. It is as though I must do something that I have never done before! Maybe at the end of this journey I will find out.

I need to go to the surface for air, and I need to see if I am nearing my journey's end. Yes! I can see something in the distance. It looks very much like the moving ground that I can remember from long ago. Only I don't feel afraid of those creatures that were attacking us when I was much, much smaller!

I shall stay swimming on the surface until I reach the water's edge, then I shall... Aaargh! What's hit me? Oh no, one of my flippers is bleeding! It looks bad, and its hurting, really hurting! I must make it to where the water ends. The water around me is turning red, please let me make it. I feel confused, I must clear my head, need all my remaining strength now, just one more push and I will be out of the water. I've made it! Now to pull myself along. I'm still bleeding, and I feel very weak now, but I know what I must do, nothing else matters, not even me. I need to find a place to dig before I am too weak to do anything! This looks a safe spot, I must dig as fast as I possibly can, and bury what I know now are eggs, my eggs! Nearly done, just push some more of this moving ground over my eggs, and I am finished. Now I must try to reach the water again. The pain I feel now is getting too much now. I think it's all over for me, I have lost too much blood, I cannot go any further, I'm done! I feel very drowsy, and I can hardly keep my eyes open.

"Yannis, Yannis, it's over here. Quick, it looks as though it has lost a lot of blood. The poor thing, what do you think happened to it, Yannis?"

"A boat's propeller, no doubt. We must stop the bleeding or she will certainly die."

Oh no, I don't want to die! Please Yannis whatever you are, help me, don't let me die.

"We must get her to the sanctuary as fast as we possibly can. Her eyes have closed, she is close to death."

Time went by. Yannis nursed the turtle day and night. Then, when everyone thought that they had lost the fight, the turtle's eyes opened slowly. Confused, she looked around her. She did not know where she was, but she knew that she was alive. Yannis stroked her head. "Welcome back, my friend." The turtle could not answer back to this strange creature, but understood that it had saved her life.

She stayed with Yannis until the time that she would be ready for the sea, and the long journey that she would once again face. As Yannis took her back to the water's edge, he told the turtle that her eggs would be safe. The turtle seemed to understand, and smiled at Yannis. In return, Yannis smiled back. As the turtle entered the water, she turned her head for one last look at the creature that had saved her life. She will never forget the creature called Yannis. Then she slipped into the water and was gone.

I hope that this story has helped to imagine a little of what a turtle has to go through, and can now understand more about what Yannis Vardakastanis is trying to achieve, saving the turtles and indeed other wildlife from an early extinction. A lot of the dangers, as I have said before, come from man, and they can be easily rectified by simply caring for the island of Zakynthos.

Rubbish that is discarded is not the only enemy of these wonderful creatures – we all know that – there are other dangers that these creatures have to face, but these are natural dangers. We cannot do anything about that, though, other than our part. Then we can preserve these creatures, and all the beautiful wildlife that exists around us.

If you see plastic bags in the water, or on the beach, pick them up and put them in a bin. This goes for plastic bottles, oil containers that get washed up, glass bottles, and, of course, discarded fish netting. Believe me, everything helps. Turtles get tangled up in this and drown. By doing simple things, we can preserve the wildlife a little longer.

What Yannis Vardakastanis does is a credit to the island of Zakynthos. His whole life is dedicated to preserving the wildlife here. He is not interested in recognition in any way. He just wants to keep this island's wildlife stable. No doubt he will continue to the day he dies.

I am grateful to him that he has allowed me and gave me the honour of writing this book. I have made a good friend, and he is someone that I will always respect.

IF THERE IS NO ROOM FOR NATURE, THEN WHAT WILL BECOME OF NATURE!

ILLEGAL HUNTING
ON ZAKYNTHOS

Illegal hunting is most certainly a problem on the island. In autumn especially, the sound of shotguns and rifle fire can be heard in every direction. I'm not against shooting for food, or if the animals are growing in numbers at such a rate that it is needed to keep the population at a healthy level so that the others can have a better chance of surviving.

This happens in other countries. My own country of England, as an example, the New Forest in the south of England, near to where I lived, has to do this yearly. The forest has wild ponies that roam the forest freely. It is indeed unfortunate that these lovely animals need to be culled, or rounded up and sent to an abattoir in France, the term meaning 'slaughterhouse'. We also do the same to deer, but we eat the meat, so it does become a food source. It is unfortunate, but by doing this it helps maintain the balance for the deer and ponies that rely on the food that the forest has to offer to sustain and ensure their survival. On occasions, I have no doubt that some animals in Zakynthos are shot for their meat – birds, rabbits, etc. – but if most people are shooting just for shootings sake, then there won't be too much left to shoot at in years to come, and the island will be almost empty of wildlife.

In England the Forest Commission are the only ones to be allowed to shoot, but these animals are carefully chosen. Maybe they are too old and will not last another winter. These animals, though, are shot by a professional marksman. Clay pigeon shooting is a popular way of shooting, a very enjoyable pastime that a lot of countries like to participate in, including myself when I lived in England.

Sadly, though, the indiscriminate shooting on this island is almost insane! Birds like the golden oriole, buzzard, and falcons are shot just for trophies! The golden oriole is a fairly secretive bird that likes to inhabit grapevines. They are not that big of a bird, and it is a complete wonder that there is anything left of the bird when it is blasted by shotgun fire! I can understand to a certain extent the shooting of pigeons if it has become a problem for the farmer, but the turtle dove – which is part of the pigeon family – is also being shot. This bird has been shot at for centuries; it is sad to know that these birds are very much in decline, and should be considered an endangered species on Zakynthos.

The local authorities seem to be a bit lackadaisical with this problem. One day, when there is not a bird in the sky, they might decide to realise their error!

Some of the hunters do not seem to recognise the dangers of shooting too near houses. I have had first-hand experience with this several times. Sitting outside the house on the balcony can be dangerous, as they seem to think that their close-quarter shots cannot possibly harm anyone. I have heard gunshot ripping through the trees next to my house, trees that are in my garden! Shot raining down on my television dish is also commonplace. This, once again, is an insane act! If they injured, or worse, killed someone because of this insane stupidity, would they have any regrets? Surely there must be a law that demands a safe distance from any dwelling! Is that also ignored? It might seem that I am picking on these so-called hunters, and if I don't like it, go back to England.

There are a lot of islanders that think the same as myself, I am thankful to say, and like me would like to see illegal hunting completely banned, and maybe the wildlife on this island would stay intact!

In forests, the hunters' presence is very noticeable by the amount of rubbish that is strewn over the forest floor. Plastic bottles, lead shot, and empty cartridges are found lying everywhere. If a glass bottle is discarded, then this could be very dangerous to the life that depends on the forest. Forest fires obviously can be caused by this, devastating great amounts of wildlife, not forgetting the firefighters that put their lives at risk pointlessly. I'm not just talking about birds, but other animals of the forest. Reptiles, such as snakes and lizards, that cannot escape the intense heat of a forest fire, so they perish, thus leaving the future of these animals in considerable danger in an instant! Let's not forget the insects of the forest that can be put into an instant state of devastation as well. Ant nests, better known as formicaries, could be wiped out! Imagine how long it would take for the forest to be able to sustain a healthy wildlife again. All this from one discarded glass bottle!

It was October 2000, the headlands above Gerakas beach were devastated by fire. As it was October, it is hard to imagine how the fire started. Possibly it could have been pranksters messing with fire, which got seriously out of control. A lighted cigarette, maybe a glass bottle that magnified the rays of the autumn sun. Whatever the cause, it had a devastating effect.

The wildlife in that area was almost, as you can imagine, wiped out! You really cannot wonder about Yannis Vardakastanis' frustrations. This man is tireless in his commitment to preserve all wildlife on this island. Turtles, I think I have already said, are his main passion. If there were a hundred people on this island that could give the same amount of effort as Yannis, I don't think this island would have a problem.

The mixed pine forest of the Vasilikos Peninsula provides an important sanctuary for migratory and resident birds.

In the year 2000, Earth, Sea & Sky volunteers helped Yannis clear tonnes of rubbish from the forest's interior. Yannis explained to me that the rubbish was such a huge amount that the forest floor looked like a plastic carpet! Can you imagine what that looked like! It certainly would have an extreme effect on the wildflowers that grow there, not to mention the wildlife. It must have been like walking through a rubbish tip. The danger of fire would have been made even more of a threat"

RUBBISH COLLECTED IN YEAR 2000 IN VASILIKOS PENINSULA

There are 425 different bird species recorded in Greece, 243 of these are native and obviously breed in the country. So bird life is pretty healthy. Most of these birds are found in the mountainous regions. For the island of Zakynthos, it is not so healthy. Yes, there are birds here, and, yes, their numbers are fairly healthy and it is a pleasure to go bird watching, but with the shooting – and they seem to shoot at anything – the birds will one day vanish, or at least diminish to such a level that the bird songs that we enjoy will be harder to find. This would be a crying shame, birds are beautiful creatures, we don't want this heaven to be destroyed out of pure stupidity!

BIRDS THAT CAN BE
SPOTTED ON THE ISLAND

Some of the birds that you may see here are really lovely. Take the woodchat shrike; loves vineyards, gardens and marquis landscapes. This is a really lovely bird. The colouration of this bird is very distinctive with its rust-coloured head, white shoulders, blackish above and pure white below with a thick band of black that runs across the face above the beak and around the eyes. The great grey shrike, and the lesser grey shrike, also can be found here. They are both black, grey and white, however the great grey shrike has a thinner black band across the eyes. I have spotted all three of these birds and it certainly made my day more pleasurable.

The Sardinian warbler is resident to the island, has a black head, white throat and red eye-ring, and, as I have said before, this bird is one of my favourites.

The golden oriole; this is the one they shoot for trophies! The male a stunning yellow with black wings and tail. The female of the species is green and yellow. It can be confused with the green woodpecker. I have so far never seen a green woodpecker here, so I am not sure if these birds are resident.

I have spoken about the Eleanora's falcon, but these birds are unique in Greece, as two-thirds of the world's population breed in Greece. This in itself would be a good reason to support these majestic birds.

The island of Zakynthos and the rest of Greece must realise that these birds are not here for hunting pleasure and realise how lucky they are to have these birds. I can go on all night about the different birds on this island, but I don't want to begin to bore you. I will say to you, if your interest in birds was only half as much as my own passion for these superb creatures, you would see a very different world, one that you would never want to end. It would also stop the senseless shooting that these creatures have to endure from illegal hunters.

SOME EXAMPLES OF THE BEAUTIFUL FLOWERS THAT GROW ON
THE ISLAND. THERE ARE MANY, ALL IN DIFFERENT COLOURS AND
THERE ARE FLOWERS IN ABUNDANCE FOR EVERY SEASON.

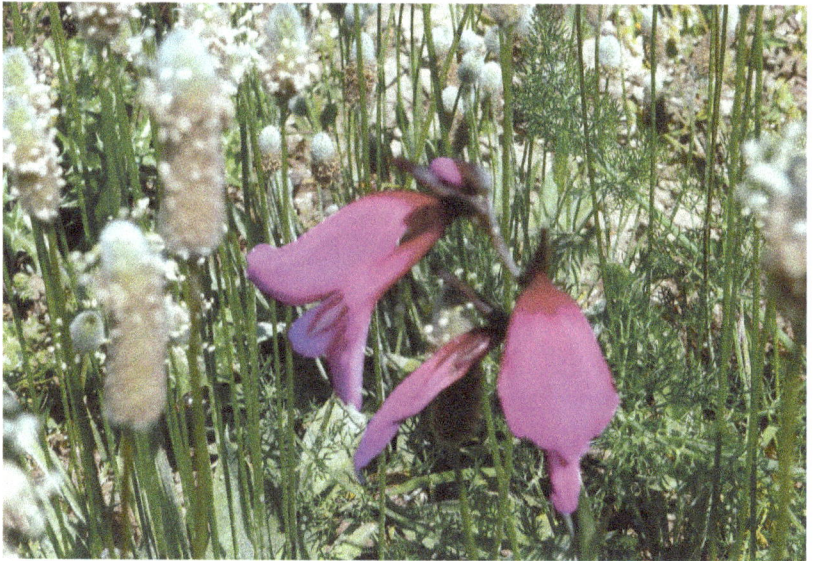

FLORA AND FAUNA
ON THE ISLAND

Some of the flower species that can be seen on Zakynthos grow in abundance. The sea daffodil that can be seen growing on the beaches and sand dunes around the island certainly are. The flower will bloom between August and September. This flower is superb and is the favourite of Yannis, but although this plant is healthy in numbers, its survival can be threatened by tourists sometimes as the plant is of a bulbous kind and some are dug up so that they can take them back home. The flower can be seen all around the island, but it seems to prefer the southern parts of the island's beaches. More so Gerakas, Banana beach, and more notably, Kalamaki. They are strewn everywhere on this beach. The leaves are of course like the normal daffodil and the colour of the flower is white. They are unmistakable, and certainly on Kalamaki there is vast numbers that grow all along the sand banks. They are not a tall flower, but in numbers give a nice display.

The cyclamen, also known amusingly in Zakynthos as 'kopelitas', as the flower resembles a little girl wearing a frilly skirt. This plant can also be seen all over the island. It is a pink/light purple colour. There are two species of this plant found in Greece, and it appears around October just after the first rain. A lovely flower that gives a grand display, I like to see them growing on mounds or banks as their beautiful blooms tend to stand out perfectly to the eye.

There certainly are an array of flowers on the island, lots of yellows of different shades, orange, white, like the lovely simple daisy, a real favourite of mine, superb in its simplicity. These daisies grow in large amounts and give a most spectacular sight. Other colours are red and pink, mauve and lilac, I could go on for ages, but I think that you have got the picture by now. However,

I must tell you about the lily, pure white in colour and big leaves that narrow at the end. This superb plant would grace anywhere. It grows near water and is in abundance. It flowers in March and into April, so it will not be seen by too many tourists. My wife nicknamed it the funeral flower, which very correctly is used for funerals.

In the winter the island is a yellow wonderland. They are everywhere, in the olive groves the floor is carpeted with them, and the open meadows. What fascinates me, is the small dykes that are either side of some of the roads. These dykes in the summer are very dry, and would probably would be overlooked by most people as uninteresting, but to me, in the winter months these dykes are full of running crystal-clear rain water. This is where they come into their own. Plantation springs up from the dykes' beds, making a beautiful carpet of submerged plant life of many different species. It is magical watching as the plants gradually grow in the running waters. I Like to think that this is a secretive part of the island , that only myself will constantly enjoy!

Everywhere on this island has great beauty, whether it's the wildlife or the plant life. It's no wonder that Yannis Vardakastanis wants to preserve all this wonderful nature that gracefully surrounds the island.

With help, this island can be a wonderland. The loggerhead turtle could possibly be the animal version of ambassador for the island's survival, as long as we allow it to survive, itself.

KERI LAKE

This is a real place of interest. Right behind the beach is the lake of Keri, which is surrounded by hills all way around. The lake is full of reeds, making the lake almost impossible to see. Only small areas of water can be seen, and in full summer, none. There is a stream that runs around the valley, which is full of life. Birds are plentiful; warblers, wagtails, goldfinch, buntings, the list goes on. I go birdwatching regularly with my wife, Maureen. Birds of prey are a delight; eagles, buzzards, falcons, and even marsh harriers, all cruising majestically in the skies above the lake, diving and flying in a circular fashion. To walk around the lake is a real pleasure. The small stream that runs around this small valley has its own interests, such as the frogs, which can be seen, and certainly heard; their call is unmistakable. The colour of them is a bright green with black spots running along their backs. Of course, not to mention the terrapins that breed in the stream would be indeed a crime. There are two types, but one which has a lighter back are now rare. Shoals of fish that swim back and forth in different sizes show just how clean the running water is in this liquid paradise.

Walking around this lovely oasis certainly has its rewards, if you are lucky, you may see a snake sunbathing on some of the rocks, which are scattered amongst the reeds. It only takes about twenty minutes to walk around the area, but if you are like me, then it will probably take an hour or two! You will certainly see terrapins sunbathing, but they are very shy, so do a bit of tiptoeing; it will certainly be worth the effort.

Swifts and swallows migrate here in spring, and they will display their arrival by flying all round the valley, and at very low levels, sometimes as little as six inches off the ground. This they do over the sea also, so it is a spectacular sight. Last year, as they were getting ready to leave the island for the winter months, I watched a falcon swooping down on them from a great height. I could not identify the falcon properly, but I was pretty confident that it was a peregrine, not sure it was successful though.

As I have said earlier, there is a lot to see here, and I would wish this lovely place to stay in its healthy state and enjoy all the wildlife that lives here. Yannis Vardakastanis certainly does, and with the support that is needed to retain this paradise, we can all enjoy it for years to come.

THERE ARE TWO TYPES OF TERRAPIN IN KERI, ONE OF THEM IS VERY RARE.
WE WERE LUCKY ENOUGH TO BE ABLE TO GET A GOOD PHOTO OF BOTH SPECIES
SUNBATHING. THE TERRAPIN IS JUST AS HAPPY OUT OF WATER AS IT IS IN.
THE PICTURE BELOW IS OF A FROG THAT ALSO LIVES VERY HAPPILY AMONG
THE TERRAPIN. IT IS A BEAUTIFUL GREEN COLOUR WITH BLACK SPOTS,
BUT THE CALL TO OTHER FROGS IS VERY LOUD, AND CERTAINLY UNMISTAKABLE.

THE REALISATION OF RUBBISH

I know I have spoken about the rubbish problem, and the effect it can have on the planet, let alone the island! Each year 6.5 billion kilos of plastic waste gets into the oceans!

This amount is very hard to believe, but the fact is that it is true! Plastics take between 100 to 1000 years to degrade. The rubbish is transported along gutters, etc., which in turn enter into the rivers, which then lead into the oceans. This plastic waste enters the oceans at an incredible rate of an unbelievable 206 kilos per second. A large amount of this waste sinks and ends up on the ocean beds. A considerable amount, though, remains floating on the ocean's surface forming a plastic soup! In the Pacific, apparently, there is what's called a plastic continent. I have never heard of this myself, but I have been told that it is as large as Manhattan! Worse still, I have read in a magazine that it is five times as big as France!

I can only assume that one of them is correct, but can you imagine how many square miles that is! If this is true the whole world should be ashamed. All this could be averted, just by putting waste in its appropriate place. Of course, Zakynthos' rubbish problem looks minute to the waste that is in the Pacific, but needless to say, it is still a concern.

Rubbish on Kalamaki beach. Although the beach seems to have been cleaned of plastic and other waste a bit more this year, 2015, and looks a lot tidier than last winter, it could still be better. Amongst the sand dunes there are plastic bottles and containers laying everywhere, and near the small marshes that still remain there are piles of plastic bottles which, you can imagine, are not good for the wildlife that live there. This being a marine park area does not give total confidence in their approach in sustaining the creatures' survival expectations!

I found recently a 40-gallon drum on the beach nearing the Crystal beach area. This almost certainly was washed up by the tide, its cap was separated from the drum and diluted oil from the salt waters was seeping from it. The label on the drum said 'toxic'. I returned some nine days later to find the offending article still laying there, minus its contents. This, one can only assume, had been drained into the sands. The drum had been moved around and jumped on, leaving large dents in the drum's body. An article of concern, and certainly not good for the environment! We must do better. Let's keep this wonderful island safe for all the wildlife, flora and fauna that depends on this habitat.

I have spoken to some tourists that come over here; some are regular visitors. They have concerns also, not just about the wildlife but of the interior of Zakynthos town itself, with all the graffiti that is sprayed on some of the buildings. Surely it would be better for the residents and tourists if we adopted a more acceptable approach and got rid of this pointless defacing, and punish the people that cause it. I know this is not about wildlife, or Yannis Vardakastanis for that matter, and I am sure that he will forgive me for mentioning it – it is more of a personal note that I felt had to be mentioned.

PLANT LIFE IN GREECE

In Greece there are 6000 different plant species, and 700 of these are endemic, meaning that they occur nowhere else in the world. So Greece is pretty unique. That alone should be enough to make all Greeks feel proud of that fact. Yannis Vardakastanis certainly is, and it's for this sort of reason, at least on the island of Zakynthos, that he will continue his fight for the preservation of all wildlife, flora and indeed fauna. The truth of the matter is that we all have our part to play if we wish to continue living in a paradise.

THE SANCTUARY AT GERAKAS

This was the dream that became reality for Yannis Vardakastanis in 1993. The starting of the sanctuary was helped by no other than HRH Prince Charles, with his Prince's Trust, giving the amount of £1500. This of course was not only an honour for Yannis, but, more importantly, the foundations to get him started.

Yannis had helped organize the transportation of three turtles that were injured, and were sent to England with the help of Archelon. It was very unfortunate that two of them did not survive, but one did, and is still alive today happily living out its life in safe captivity.

Because of this selfless act, Sea Life started to sponsor Yannis. It took a while though, taking from 2001 to 2006 before Sea Life agreed to support Yannis. In 2001 the sanctuary SOS Save Our

Sea Turtles was born. In 2006, Yannis started to build a more structural sanctuary in Laganas with concrete. This he did until 2011, five years later, when he abandoned the project, as, for some unknown reason, Marine Park decided not to be happy with the erection of this building, and were making things very awkward for Yannis. As I said, I have no idea why. Why would they try and prevent him? The local people were not giving any support either! Surely they could see sense in a sanctuary; are they not interested in the saving of turtles, or any wildlife for that matter? Was this just something that would affect them financially? As for Marine Life, I would have thought they would welcome it with open arms. At the moment, any injured turtles have to be transported to Athens, and, as I think I said before, this journey takes eight hours. So why stop a man that wants to ensure the turtles of Zakynthos that get injured have somewhere nearer? This can only enhance their survival! What Marine Life did do, though, was to create a vast debt for Yannis. Yannis was sickened by their selfish efforts to stop him building in Laganas and went back to Gerakas.

Earth, Sea & Sky

April 4, 2015

Elana Oser

Through an alternative break program at the College of Charleston (*CofC*) in South Carolina I had the incredible opportunity to volunteer for Earth, Sea & Sky in the summer of 2014. I flew to Greece, and embarked on one of the most life-changing adventures of my life. This experience is what drives me today to pursue working as marine conservationist.

The few months prior to arriving at Earth, Sea & Sky, I, and the other nine volunteers from *CofC*, learned as much as we possibly could about tourism and the devastation it is causing marine habitats. However, when I first arrived I quickly realized that I still had a lot to learn. Yannis and Jonna worked hard to continue educating my group, and train us to teach tourists. While teaching us, I was awestruck by the passion Yannis and Jonna have for their work. Their strength to fight for the survival of marine wildlife, and promote sustainable tourism was incredible to be exposed to.

My experience with Earth, Sea & Sky truly changed me. I always had a love for the environment; however, it was not until I met Yannis and Jonna that I felt like I could go into conservation. They constantly face obstacles and hardships, yet their passion for their work is enough to allow them continue fighting. This makes them incredibly unique, and I find myself aspiring to have half of the strength that they demonstrate. I find myself constantly thinking about my time as a volunteer, and am itching to continue working in marine conservation. This organization inspired me to not only to pursue a profession in conservation, but to also change my own lifestyle.

I no longer attend *CofC* and am now a student at the George Washington University (*GWU*) in Washington, DC. I am so excited to continue my work with Earth, Sea & Sky, and see my transferring as a wonderful opportunity to connect another university with this organization. It is my hope to start a student group at *GWU* that raises money for Earth, Sea & Sky, and to educate the student body to raise awareness about sustainable tourism, and marine habitat conservation.

Ultimately, it is my goal for *GWU's* alternative break program to give even more students an opportunity to volunteer with the organization that inspired me to fight for the environment. Earth, Sea & Sky has a very special place in my heart. I want to do everything I can to give back to the organization that gave so much to me.

THE BIG TANK AREA THAT'S SHOWN BEING WORKED ON WILL HOUSE FOUR LARGE TANKS THAT WILL HOLD AN ASTOUNDING 25 TONNES OF SEA WATER IN EACH TANK.

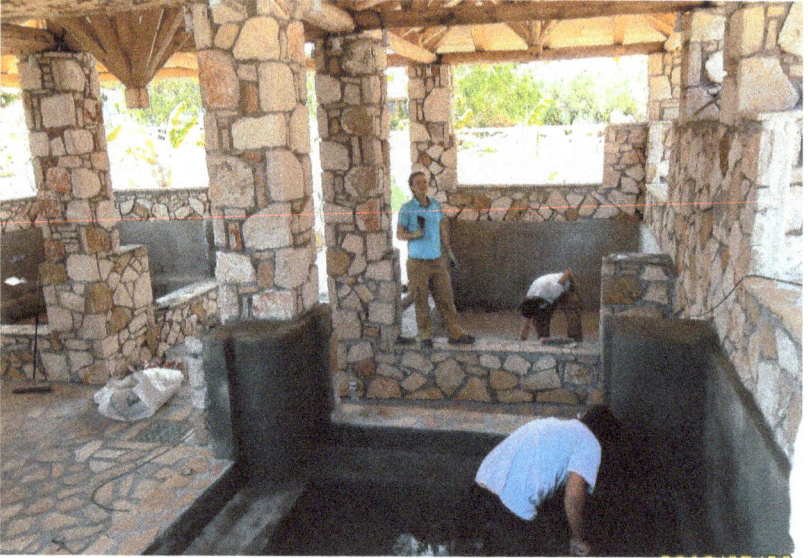

THE OUTSIDE OF THE SAME BUILDING, WITH NO EXPENSE SPARED. THE TANKS INSIDE ARE NOW READY TO ACCOMMODATE INJURED TURTLES.

Yannis Vardakastanis is not a man to give up, and after a while started to build again, this time in Gerakas, his area of birth. In 2011, he started to build a concrete structure with a stone fascia. With the support of Earth, Sea & Sky, and his own money, he employed two Albanians to help with the huge task that lay ahead. The days were long and hard, working under the pressure of the island's hot sun, and during the sometimes windy conditions of winter he strived forward. The work took all his time up, and trying to run his business as well was taking its toll. Marine Life were no more helpful than before, and tried to make it difficult for Yannis, but this time they would not deter Yannis. As I have said, this man was determined and there would be no more defeat in his mind.

Slowly the building started to take shape. Of course there were problems; money was the most notable, and as he had to pay wages, it was not all worry-free. There were volunteers, too, that helped, most notably with the four big tanks that are in another separate building from the main. The structure of the tanks had to be built of very strong laminated glass. The glass for all four of the tanks came at a cost of £6000, as they had to contain about 25 tonnes of water. I have no idea how many gallons they hold each, but the pressure must be enormous. That's 100 tonnes of water in all; I think there must have been some concerns about the glass being able to withstand the pressure! The sanctuary took about four years to complete, although there was much more that Yannis wanted to build, but that would come in time. The cost to run the tanks is about £3000 per year. Yannis built more tanks that sit behind the main building, 10 in all. These are for the unfortunate hatchlings that get injured as they make their way to the water's edge, I believe. Yannis has told me that they need to be able to have enough tanks for up to 10 young turtles, which is a rule of a sanctuary.

The volunteers are very regular every year, coming from all over the world. America, England, Japan, Scotland, New Zealand, etc. They make it easier for Yannis and for Jonna Pederson, who has now become the project manager for the sanctuary full-time. Jonna, who hails from Denmark, but has a remarkable American accent, started as a volunteer at the sanctuary and worked there for four weeks then for six weeks. Jonna was and is playing a big part for the sanctuary. Jonna, a zoo keeper by profession, has dealt with all kind of animals, and worked in mainland Greece for some time. She has, however, been around a good part of the world as a zookeeper and conservationist. Jonna certainly knows her stuff, as she has worked with rhino, big cats, dolphins, snakes. In fact, you name it, she has probably worked with it, of course not to mention turtles. Conservation is very important to her, but it was the turtles of Zakynthos that seemed to be more appealing to her. After her volunteer work with Yannis, she went back to the zoo, but because of her appeal for the loggerhead turtle she came back and took the project manager's job that Yannis offered her.

Jonna does her job very well; she organises the volunteers' jobs and helps them with their projects that they want to create for the sanctuary. Jonna is the only paid member, but this is only for the open season of the sanctuary, which is from the beginning of May to the end of October. Yannis is very lucky to have her on his team, but even he knows she is no pushover, and she will tell him if she does not agree with some things that he might do! Jonna knows that sometimes Yannis can be stubborn but she has a way of putting him right. I am very pleased to say, though, that Jonna and Yannis have become a couple. They are very suited to each other, and I think that this is going to be a big asset to the sanctuary, although Yannis may not know it yet!

I have said that Jonna deals with the volunteers, but she also has to do all the clerical work and sometimes run the shop within the sanctuary, plus maybe a bit of cleaning also. My wife and I have become good friends with Jonna and, of course, Yannis and we too are part-time volunteers.

Yannis' days are very long and there's not too much time for relaxing as he has to be up very early in the morning to check the beaches, and he works 'til about 11 at night, so he is grateful for all the help he can get. It is unfortunate that his family do not really understand his passion, but that does not deter him in the slightest.

Inside the sanctuary is worth a look. There are many more tanks there, some very big. Of course, if you do not see any turtles in them don't despair as this is a good thing. It means that there are no turtles injured. Yannis recently rescued a number of fish from the river that runs into the sea at Laganas. The river was drying up through the summer's heat. Yannis saved around 2500 fish from a grizzly death. These fish are now swimming happily in the tanks of the sanctuary, after using only a small fishnet and plastic container to bring them to the sanctuary. This was indeed no small task as he could only catch a few at a time, as they would die of stress and lack of oxygen. So there were many trips to be made. This, though, would not deter someone like Yannis Vardakastanis. Although he saved so many, he was upset that he could not save more. Now he has to pay for food for them all from his own pocket, but as I have said before, this is what this extraordinary man is all about

The fish will be released when the time is right, so they could be his guests for a while to come. The sanctuary has a shop and sells an assortment of things, including some singular stories written by myself about Yannis the turtle. All money raised from these goes to the running of the sanctuary. There is a snake called Diamond that is resident in the sanctuary. It is not dangerous, so don't be too alarmed. Sometimes you may see Yannis or the volunteers giving Diamond its daily constitutional.

Although the clinic that has just been recently finished is ready to take any unfortunate turtle that has been injured, it has to wait for the appropriate papers to be signed, which can take a little time. The sanctuary has many organisations interested, and they come from all over the world. An American organisation that, most years, sends some of its members over to the sanctuary to learn more about the turtle could not make it in 2014, but what they did do was to offer Yannis Vardakastanis and Jonna Pederson a chance to go over to America at the cost of the of the American organisation, which they both accepted with open arms. They both told me that it really opened their eyes. The conservation over there is nothing short of first class, and they both learned a tremendous amount from this amazing trip.

In 2015, there was another visitor from America. There was a conference in Turkey during the same year. Yannis and Jonna could not make the conference due to commitments at the sanctuary. One of the people who attended the conference had heard about Yannis' sanctuary in Zakynthos, and was interested in paying a visit. Tommy Cutt, chief conservation officer for the Loggerhead Marine Life Centre in Florida was invited by Yannis to come and stay and check out the sanctuary. He stayed for two weeks. He could not believe what Yannis had done in such a short time! He was nothing short of impressed. In those two weeks, they had learned a lot from each other, even myself and Maureen, my wife, had been enlightened! This was to prove beneficial for the sanctuary, as now it has a very powerful organisation behind their efforts to conserve the turtles and the wildlife that is in Zakynthos.

Outside the sanctuary at the entrance, you will see a giant turtle. Don't be alarmed; it's a model. The turtle is about five metres in length, two metres high, and about four metres in width. Its name is Zantos, and it was completely blue, so it was time for a makeover. The colours used were to make it more appealing to the visitors, and I had the privilege to paint it for Yannis.

The fields across from the sanctuary are full of wildlife. The flowers are amazing, all colours; reds, yellows of every shade, blues, white. It really is incredible. There are many species of butterflies and the insects are also fascinating. Birds, including birds of prey, are also a common sight. It is no wonder that Yannis built the sanctuary here, he could not have picked a better place.

I feel at peace when I visit this place. Yannis was, as I have said, born here, and I envy his birthplace, this wondrous Shangri-La.

Yannis received three awards for his efforts in conservation. One in 2005, one in 2007 and another in 2009. A remarkable achievement for one man in that short space of time. These were awarded by tourist companies, no mean feat for anyone.

The sanctuary was a dream for Yannis for years, and in 2011, the season started off with a 'mascot' for the rescue centre. Courtesy of sea life centres, Paul, the oracle octopus of the world cup, was chosen to represent the sea turtle rescue project, thus helping the sanctuary raise an amazing amount of 100,000 euros to continue the work still needed to complete the centre. Posters and boards were displayed by the sea life centres across the UK and Europe as part of the campaign.

Sadly, Paul passed away on the 26th October to the chagrin of his keepers at Oberhausen Sea Life, as well as his many fans from all over the world who were inspired and indeed delighted by his psychic talents!

This, though, did not deter the volunteers, who were skilled in building, to come from all over the world to help with the completion of the sanctuary, which was planned to be completed in early 2011. The light at the end of the tunnel was now very evident.

In 2010, the NMPZ (National Marine Park Zakynthos) suffered from severe financial cuts during the 2010 season, with only 18 staff in their employ to warden beaches and for administration, compared to the 70 or 80 in previous years. Most evenings throughout the summer a lack of Marine Park presence was evident on the beaches, it was very hard for them to do their job as they would have liked as the monetary support was not available. On several occasions, tourists and vehicles were witnessed trespassing onto the nesting beaches at night time, potentially causing serious disturbance to female turtles attempting to lay their eggs. This was something that Yannis Vardakastanis was very worried about. Myself and my wife, Maureen, were also concerned as several times we had witnessed people running up and down where the nests were, playing football! The beach was in a complete state of turmoil, tourists plunging parasols into the sand not knowing whether there was a nest below, horses being ridden up and down the beach where the nests were. There were big holes left in the sand, which is another danger to the hatchlings and sandcastles were still standing proudly erect. What a disaster! How can Marine Park have any chance of finding new nests when people are not taking care for the safety of the eggs!

This has to change. Archelon try their best, but they are volunteers who oversee the beaches in the evening, but their job becomes much harder if everyone is trampling on the nesting areas. Volunteers do a good job; they are interested in what they do and they have to finance themselves to do it. They study wildlife in their home countries for the purpose of preserving all wildlife. This is something that we should all be proud of. If they continue, it is certainly going to become an asset to the future of the loggerhead and indeed all wildlife that we have on this planet.

Yannis Vardakastanis, I know, is very proud of the many volunteers that he welcomes to his sanctuary every year. Every day, Yannis learns something from them, and, in return, deposits knowledge that will be a great asset to them in the future.

Going back to the year 2010, the total number of nests in Laganas Bay was 1053, and it was a relief to all involved to note that this number was up compared to 2008 and 2009. Most notably, the nest numbers at Gerakas beach doubled in 2010. This represented the highest number of nests on Gerakas beach ever to be recorded at this time.

The up-to-date figures, however, are not so good. I think in 2013 the nests certainly started to show a decline, unfortunately, as did 2014. In 2015, in Gerakas and Sekania, the nests do not seem to be too bad. So far, there seems to be about 17 or so nests on Gerakas, and I am informed that Sekania beach seems to be in a healthy state for nesting turtles.

However, the nests on Kalamaki beach are very few! I have counted very few, four to be precise. I don't know if there are any more near the Crystal beach area. His lack of nests can be very worrying, but I do wonder if the turtles have decided to take their eggs to Sekania instead. This would not surprise me at all, as there are sunbeds as far as the eye can see.

The graph below shows the total nest numbers for each year since 1984, with what are considered the natural 'peaks and troughs'. Yet it is very clear that the peaks are getting conspicuously lower, and further apart, as the years have gone by. This, as I have just said, shows up in the latter years.

Total nests' number

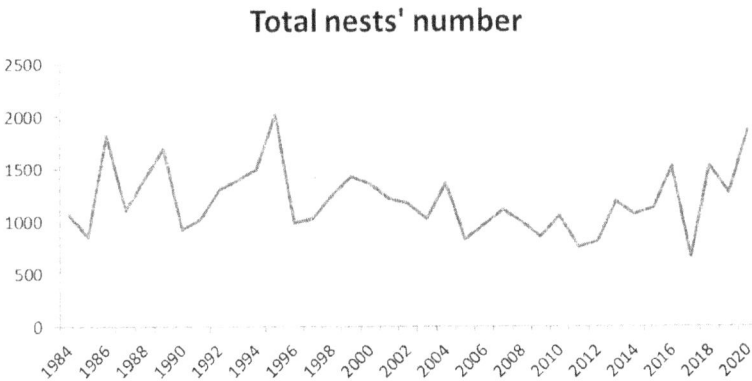

TOTAL NESTS IN LAGANAS BAY, ZAKYNTHOS

During the 2010 season, there was another increase. This time it was turtle strandings in and around the National Marine Park area, with the number of dead turtles being the highest ever recorded in one season, thus creating much concern about the need for stricter regulation of sea activities.

A total of 38 turtles were reported stranded. An injured female, tangled in discarded fishing line, was discovered in the early morning on Gerakas beach. The remaining 37 were not as fortunate as they were all to be found dead in the bay or washed up on the beaches. Exact cause of death is often difficult to determine due to varying degrees of decomposition. However, most of the deaths were brought about by human activities and interaction, the majority being incidental catch in fishing gear, or only too often, by boat strikes and pollution.

YOU CAN HELP

Use biodegradable or reusable bags instead of plastic. As I have said, plastic bags are jellyfish to a turtle, which will block its digestive system and will kill the turtle in a very unpleasant way. Also, just as important is to reduce rubbish.

If you are contemplating taking a boat out, stay within the speed limit. The speed limit within the bays is six kilometres an hour. This is very important, as the blades of the propellers are going to cause horrific injury to the unfortunate turtle that has the misfortune of getting in the blade's path. In most cases the turtle will die. If the blades hit the beak, this will once again cause a death by hunger, as it will not be able to use its beak. A death that none of us would like to see it suffer.

SOME DISCARDED FISHING NET FOUND WASHED UP ON THE BEACH

In 2010, the PADI Aware International Marine Clean-up Project saw weekly clean-ups of Gerakas beach and other nesting beaches throughout the season, collecting an estimated 500kg of debris and waste. The collection consisted mainly of plastic bottles and carrier bags, cigarette butts and around 500 glow-in-the-dark fishing lures. Volunteers in more than 100 countries tackle marine debris issues head-on. Media coverage of the project peaked mid-season with the BBC, ARD German News, and Canadian World of Wonders coming out to interview and film Yannis and his volunteers. It was exhausting, but a fun experience for all involved. 2010 seemed to be a very busy year indeed for Yannis.

Glyfada in the mainland of Greece is the only place that all the injured turtles can go. So it is the upmost of importance that a sanctuary in Zakynthos exists. I have said that the journey time for the injured turtle is about eight hours, and it is fairly obvious that not all turtles will survive the journey.

GETTING THE YOUNGER GENERATION OF ZAKYNTHOS TO BECOME AWARE OF THE WILDLIFE THAT LIVES ON THIS WONDERFUL ISLAND

I know that in time Yannis Vardakastanis wants all the young people of Zakynthos to learn and respect the wildlife, not just on this island but everywhere in the world. They must be made aware of the dangers that exist for all animals, flora, and fauna. Without these things that makes the world so beautiful, we ourselves will be in danger of dying out!

There is so much that the younger set can involve themselves in. Schools could start to do their own projects, once they have an understanding of what preservation is all about. I know that one of Yannis' wishes is to educate the young, as in time the older people will die out and make way for the young. That's how it should be, but without the proper education on all the wildlife, then it will be only a matter of time before we have nothing left. So it is very important the young know about the dangers, then it will be up to them to continue the fight for survival. We must once again remember this island of Zakynthos has, the largest amount of loggerhead turtles in the whole of Greece, something to be very proud of indeed.

Schools could organise trips to the beaches and have a clean-up day from time to time. This could be in autumn or winter. I know only too well of the difficulties in summer, as there are people on the beach relaxing and taking in the sun's rays. They can be told why they are cleaning the beaches and how important it is to wildlife that live there, explaining how it affects the sea life and the other wildlife, including the plant life. Charts could be made so that the children can keep an update of the amounts of rubbish that has been cleaned up, and what type of rubbish – tin cans, bottles, plastic bags, fishing line – and the effect it has on certain animals and plants. School outings in the summer to the sanctuary in Gerakas would allow them to learn about the loggerhead turtle. This can be simply done by phoning the sanctuary. Jonna Pedersen, the project manager for the sanctuary, I'm sure would be delighted to hear from you.

Jonna could possibly give talks to you at the schools, as I am sure Yannis Vardakastanis can. It would certainly be very rewarding for everyone. These two people are very dedicated to what they do, and the information that they can pass on to everyone will certainly be an asset to all that care to listen.

Nature walks for the children would be a great way of showing them all the plants that this island has to offer. Insects, such as the ant, have amazing skills, things that we could not possibly achieve without the use of machinery.

Butterflies, there are so many here; bees, they are so important to our survival, but this is not known to everyone, so it must be taught to the young so that they can protect them in the future. It can be a frightening thought that something so small can play a part in our own existence! Not forgetting the turtle, which has been on this planet longer than anything that lives or lived. We must give all that lives with us in this world a chance to carry on living, which in turn will help us to survive a bit longer!

The importance of what Yannis does is very evident. His passion for the preservation of wildlife cannot be competed with. Everything this man does, he does for the wildlife that he loves so much. It is no wonder that his volunteers have nothing but respect for this very rare individual.

It has been a good year (2015) so far, for myself and my wife, for spotting the loggerhead turtle. On the beach of Kalamaki, we have seen many swimming around in the bay, no doubt ready to lay their eggs, watching them pop their heads up now and again. It is as though they are checking that everything is right for them to come on to the beach. They have been very near to us sometimes, and we have had some amazing views of these fascinating creatures. I have only seen four nests on the Kalamaki beach, though, but as I have said before, the beach is not monitored 24 hours a day, so there could be many more! Yannis has assured us that there are plenty more there, but they are unmarked.

The tourists that are on the beach have also witnessed the sightings, but unfortunately, some of them try to get too close. This is no good for the turtle; I watched one family trying to surround a turtle, so that they could get a better look, and one of them was almost touching one. This, of course, is utter madness; I can understand the excitement in seeing one, we all love seeing them, but they do not realise what it is doing to the turtle. I heard another family proudly telling other people that they were trying to get around the back of a turtle so that one of them could get hold of either side of the turtle's shell and be pulled along!

This is nothing short of insanity! The turtle could get so stressed that it will drop its eggs in the sea, thus killing about 100 young. Of course, the other side of the coin could be that the turtle will bite you. People do not seem to realise that these are wild animals, and they will sometimes attack if they feel threatened in any way. The bite from a turtle could be very severe; it has a very strong beak, which could take your arm off! It's great seeing these creatures swimming in the sea, but give them the respect that they most certainly deserve.

The children can learn a lot about the turtles, and this would certainly be a benefit for them. The learning of a turtle's habits and aggressions will help them teach the children of the future. In Kalamaki there is an abundance of sea grass, which grows on the sea bed. This sea grass is a main component of the turtle's diet. In winter there are piles of sea grass washed up on the beach of Kalamaki, caused by the winter storms that attack the island. Sometimes there is that much that it's like walking on a soft mattress.

In Alykes they rarely have nestings, however two years ago my wife and I witnessed two nests. We were very surprised by this. In 2013, while swimming there, we were both delighted to see a turtle pop its head up from the sea. It was not that far away and we could see very clearly its shell that was reflecting in the sunshine. We were very selfish in keeping it to ourselves. Clearly there were bathers in the water, but we did not want to draw attention to this lone turtle, so we were very careful not to make it obvious to others that there was a turtle in their midst. Yes, I know it was selfish, but I think maybe the turtle was obliged! This does make me wonder, though, maybe there are nests in Alykes that nobody knows about at all. I just hope that if there are, then they are lucky enough to hatch and not get trodden on and crushed by people that have no idea of their existence.

A VERY REAL
WORLDWIDE PROBLEM

The future of our planet is in very great danger, not just the turtles of Zakynthos, but every turtle in the world. This also applies to every living thing. Most of this is, I am sad to say, caused by man! I will give you some examples in a moment, but most of the planet's destruction is caused by greed! The greed for money and more money is a great concern, and should be for everybody. Most of the planet's demise is caused by this 'must-have-more' attitude!

Remember, when the last tree is cut down, the last of the fish eaten, the last stream poisoned, we will then realise that we cannot eat money! It is a very worrying thought but nevertheless very true.

I would like to give some perfect examples of the planet's demise. Yes, I know it all sounds a bit over the top, and you may suggest that I sound a little bit of a mental case who needs treatment, but I can assure everyone that if we carry on like we are, then we are heading for a future living on a planet that can no longer sustain us, or anything that depends on this planet for its existence. The examples that you will read are of a grave concern, and should be to us all.

EXAMPLES

Mexico City, with its 20 million inhabitants, is destroying a vast area of land. Wildlife and people are most certainly affected by such an amount of people all living in one city.

Elephants killed for their tusks; a magnificent animal killed just because someone wishes to line their pockets with money. This should all be banned, and we know that there are armed wardens to protect these wonderful animals, but there are not enough. These poachers have no thought for the animals' agony! Sometimes the very young that have now been orphaned by these greedy savages die, and sometimes they become a target for the lion. These poachers should, as far as I am concerned, get the same treatment as they give to the animal they are killing just for a few more coins!

The rainforests, which catch fire. I know sometimes it is an accident, but this in turn affects the wildlife that depend on the forest, such as the goats that live there. Now there is no more grazing for them to be had. This in turn will help the goats deplete in big numbers, thus bringing their demise a lot closer that it should be.

Excessive air traffic throwing out emissions. This can cause so much more pollution than most of us do not realise. I know that we all use the planes, so we are all to blame, but we must find a solution to this problem before it starts to really affect us!

Oil sand is considered to be the energy source of the future, but at what cost! We have factories bellowing pollution into the air. This will cause concern if it is not dealt with. It reminds me of the 1950s when I was a boy in London. We had so much smog then, all caused by the industries. It was very hard to see anything, the fog was so thick! We wore scarves around our faces so that we did not breathe it into our lungs; it certainly was not pleasant. A lot of people were becoming ill because of it, and some would die. We had to do something, and what we did was to make everywhere a smokeless zone, and after a while London became a more healthy place to live. It seems to me, though, that we will go back to that era if nothing is done, and we can enjoy bad health once again! I understand fully that we have to find different energy sources, but not at the cost of lives, and also the wildlife that will be certainly affected by it. Let's stop this madness, and keep the air clean for the future as well.

The Yellow River in Inner Mongolia – this another problem for the planet's future. It stinks so badly that even a tough Mongolian herd farmer cannot stand the smell! Can you imagine what that smells like! With so much build-up of pollution it must be horrendous. It is easy to say it's only a river, how is that going to affect the planet, but it will as everything that is bad for this planet's existence accumulates into a massive pile of worry for the future.

An incineration plant in Bangladesh has rubbish as far as the eye can see, which is burnt; more of that foul smoke pumping its thick waste into the atmosphere.

Increased fires as a result of climate change. This is not caused by man, but by the changing of the planet. We witness this almost on a daily basis. We cannot do too much about this, but by adding man-made problems to it as well, we do not help it in any way. The world is changing, it's been changing for millions of years. Jurassic animals that lived all those millions of years ago – all but a few are still with us; crocodiles and turtles were perfectly made to adapt to this day. Sadly, these animals are in danger now because of our stupidity.

Los Angeles; the energy demand for this city is unfathomable. The lights can be clearly seen spreading for miles from space! Can you imagine how much that is taking from the planet! It is very hard to believe, but daily it is draining the planet of its natural resources.

In Oregon, a 1000-year-old forest fell victim to the chainsaw for a new dam! This forest will never see the light of day again. Why on earth does someone want to cut a 1000-year-old forest down?" Yes, they might very well need a new dam, but could they have not found another place for it? It all revolves around money, but some things are more precious than the accursed bank account to the greedy people that really do not care whatsoever about the planet as long as they have their greedy fingers wrapped around another bundle of money.

The area around Almeria in Spain is littered with greenhouses as far as the eye can see, simply for a richly filled dinner table!

Tigers – they too cannot escape man's greed for money. They are hunted for their fur, so that some rich person can boast of a rug gracing their expensive houses. Tigers are very much in decline, and we must preserve this beautiful beast, and stop all this hunting so that the rich selfish people won't be able to gloat and be proud of the fact that they are rapidly putting the tiger out of existence. Maybe they would be better hunting themselves and hanging themselves on the wall, I am sure that most of the people that live on the planet would be delighted!

Paradise almost lost – the Maldives – a very popular vacation spot that is threatened by rising sea levels. Once again, something that we can really do nothing about. There are many small islands in the Maldives that will certainly one day be lost to us. It will be a very sad day when that happens, but this is the course of nature and there is not a lot we can do about it, but of course there are other things in our power that we can do, and that we must strive for the preservation of all those things that we can do, it is very simple.

Tonnes, literally, of broken electronics end up in developing countries, and are stripped for precious metals by using deadly substances.

The blunder of the Brazilian rainforest is being repeated in Canada. Where next, the New Forest, England!

The entire world watched the events of Fukushima – a massive heat and power station was burning just a few miles away. All attempts to extinguish it were fruitless.

Disappearing ice caps are robbing polar bears of both their living space and food, causing their certain deaths. It's such a shame to see these beautiful animals becoming the victims of the unstoppable nature!

There is now a massive waterfall from melting pack ice. These masses are the only meltwater on earth and the undeniable proof of how swiftly climate change is advancing.

In Indonesia, surfers ride waves with filth and rubbish that contaminates the sea.

The prophecy is becoming a more and more brutal reality, but, even today, not every person is aware of the horrible effects our lifestyles are having on nature, and its existence!

There is talk in Australia about cutting a channel through the barrier reef, so that ships can carry coal through it! Can you imagine the devastation on the sea life that depends on the reefs for their survival. The barrier reef must be one of the wonders of the world. The world is becoming insane! Let's not care about wrecking it! As long as someone can get richer by destroying something so beautiful. This really must not happen. If we let the greedy destroy our planet for personal gain, then we deserve to lose everything. Maybe we could just live in a pile of concrete so that these people can have the lifestyle they so yearn for.

All this senseless destruction, mostly caused by one thing – man. Animals that are not party to human greed face a grim future. What gives us the right to determine their fate? If the shoe was on the other foot, we would certainly suggest that this would be extremely unfair. Selfishness and greed must be wiped out, or this planet, and us, will not survive. It seems pretty evident to me that we do not realise that we are planning our own suicide!

Yannis Vardakastanis does realise this, but he is one man, and no matter how much he does to help sustain the wildlife of his beloved Zakynthos, he cannot do it alone. He needs as much help as possible to try to preserve wildlife. Let the greedy people of this world start to do something for others for a change. Help people like Yannis and all the others around the world that want to see the wildlife survive. I am sure that these people who try desperately to save our planet from becoming a barren waste would welcome their help.

All these bad things that I have just written are perfectly true. It is certainly a concern of mine, because it's not just me but my family and every other family that will be affected by the way the world is going, and in the future surely we want things to be good for the generations to come. We live on the planet with every living thing. They are put here for a reason, and so are we. Why change it? Remember, most things are probably destroyed by money – we all need it, but we need to sustain our planet more.

CECIL THE LION

In July 2015, Cecil the lion, who was well known, was coaxed out of the safety area where he lived and was then shot by some rich American dentist. The lion was shot with a bow and arrow, which wounded him, he was then left over night to suffer before the brave hunter tracked him down the next day and shot him again with a bow and arrow, which killed Cecil.

The so-called hunter then skinned and took the lion's head so that he could have the all-important trophy! This lion had a collar on so that he could be recognised. According to our brave hunter, he did not know this and he threw the collar into the trees, hoping no one would notice it. This, however, has caused a big stir within the public, and so far has raised 100,000 signatures in protest. Mr Walter Palmer has now been named and shamed. And even his address has been displayed. He paid $37,000 to kill the lion. He also killed a rhino and a leopard, and he wanted to hunt an elephant, but they could not find one big enough for him. Nice guy.

The good thing is that the public have gone crazy. Who the hell does this man think he is, to think he is rich enough to be above the law!

If he is so desperate to kill animals, why does he not do it in a way that gives the animal a chance. Maybe if he was given a stick to hunt with, he might not be so eager. I mean he might get hurt by the animals that he so likes to kill just for sport and a trophy. I am sure that the animals hunted would accommodate him. This Walter Palmer has certainly found fame, and I hope he is proud of himself. I have the funny feeling, though, that his dentist business will flounder badly, then he will not be able to afford to kill animals for personal delight!

There was a woman recently – I do not know her name – who hunted and killed a giraffe, once again for so-called sport. She is seen in a picture very proudly standing by a dead giraffe, she must be very proud of herself.

It's people like these two specimens that the good people in the world want to be stopped!

Take someone like Johan Eliasch, a Swedish millionaire. He purchased 400,000 acres of Amazon rainforest from a logging company for $14,000,000 for the sole purpose of preservation. This sort of person deserves recognition worldwide.

Another example of goodness was from a diver in Mexico who discovered a turtle with rope tangled around one of his flippers. This was a large amount of rope that was tied to a buoy that was floating freely. The diver managed to free the turtle from its entanglement. There was minor injury, but the turtle swam away, no doubt delighted. Thanks to these kinds of people, we still have hope for the future of the wildlife that live with us on this planet.

A MENTION OF THE BEES IN THE WORLD

Bees are becoming critical. If there are no bees we must remember that there will be no oranges, no apples, no tomatoes, no onions, no kiwis, no peaches, *no people.*

THE HAWKSBILL SEA TURTLE

A new study shows how hawksbills are escaping the hottest waters of the Arabian Gulf. Sea turtles' lives are dictated, in large, by heat. Subtle temperature variations shape their embryonic development, determine their sex, and influence their growth and nesting activity. So how do the turtles respond?

Sea surface temperatures in the gulf can climb as high as 98 degrees Fahrenheit in the summer, and air temperatures as high as 122 degrees Fahrenheit. The turtles will migrate to deeper and cooler waters in response. They will then stay at this depth until the temperatures drop. In 2010, the Emirates Wildlife Society and WWF teamed up to study them.

Members of the initiative, called the Marine Turtle Conservation Project, attached satellite transmitters to 90 turtles at nesting sites in Iran and Qatar. Oman and the VAE then tracked the animals' movements. In November 2014, they announced what the transmitters revealed. Every summer, when coastal waters reached 90 degrees Fahrenheit, the hawksbill migrated to deeper waters. These findings are the first real time evidence of sea turtles changing their behaviour in order to cope with these warmer temperatures. Maybe other turtle species will respond in the same way over time. This is a good reason to encourage stronger protection for all the places these turtles need to go. The island of Zakynthos must be rated at a high protection level for the loggerheads. This is why it is so very important that we help the turtles, and not ignore them.

FIRE ON MOUNT SKOPOS

A fire broke out on Mount Skopos on 18th July 2015, possibly started by a cigarette. This is ridiculous; it is also thought that the fire was deliberate! I hope that it was just an accident, but however it started, it must have been a fireman's nightmare! Mount Skopos is flush with flora and fauna, and of course, wildlife. So this is a tragedy for the island of Zakynthos. If it was deliberate, then they put the firemen that dealt with it in great danger of losing their lives. These people are heroes that risk their lives to save property and, more so, human life. Not to lose their own lives through some brainless idiot! The fire must have been at least a kilometre in length, and the flames some 60 feet high. We must not forget, though, that this could have been caused by discarded rubbish. I am sad to say that on this island it is only too evident that people just throw plastic or glass bottles out of car windows as they drive. Surely they must realise the dangers of this causing fires!

A view from paradise
Emily McLaughlin, West Yorkshire, England
Volunteer and intern at Earth, Sea & Sky

"The wilderness holds answers to questions man has not yet learned to ask" - Nancy Newhall

I first visited the island in 2011 to volunteer with Earth, Sea & Sky. It was the summer before I moved to university to study wildlife conservation and I wanted a taste of what conservation work is really like and a chance to help protect the endangered loggerhead sea turtle. I really enjoyed my time as a volunteer here, a few weeks was just not enough! I had no idea how greatly those few weeks as a volunteer would impact my life.

Four years on and I graduated with a BSc in wildlife conservation, co-founded a wildlife conservation society in Liverpool and volunteered with a wide variety of animal welfare and environment protection organisations, but Earth, Sea & Sky was still on my mind. I kept a close eye on the development of the centre and the work they were continuing to do, until one day, lo and behold, they were in need of an intern. I applied and I was accepted.

Being the project manager's assistant for the entire season has enabled me to see so much more. The impact of the tourism industry has really hit the island hard; completely transforming it from a quiet rural island with no electricity or cars into a popular holiday destination in just a few decades. Witnessing the never-ending problems facing the wildlife here on the island, especially the sea turtles, takes its toll on you. I'll always remember the first time I visited the tourist hotspots on the island and witnessed first-hand how tourism has damaged and in some cases completely destroyed turtle nesting beaches, it didn't take long before I was moved to tears.

It breaks my heart to see such a beautiful island and its wildlife destroyed in the pursuit of money; but this only compels me to work harder to conserve and protect the island. Our most important role here is to inform the visitors about the plight of the island and to help them help us by being an environmental and turtle-friendly tourist.

I am continually blown away by the hard work, passion and dedication Yannis shows for the island and its visiting turtles year after year. Never in my life have seen someone work as hard as he does, he is truly an inspiration and has achieved so much. Earth, Sea & Sky have big plans for the future to continue expanding the project and I believe they will continue to do extraordinary work in the future.

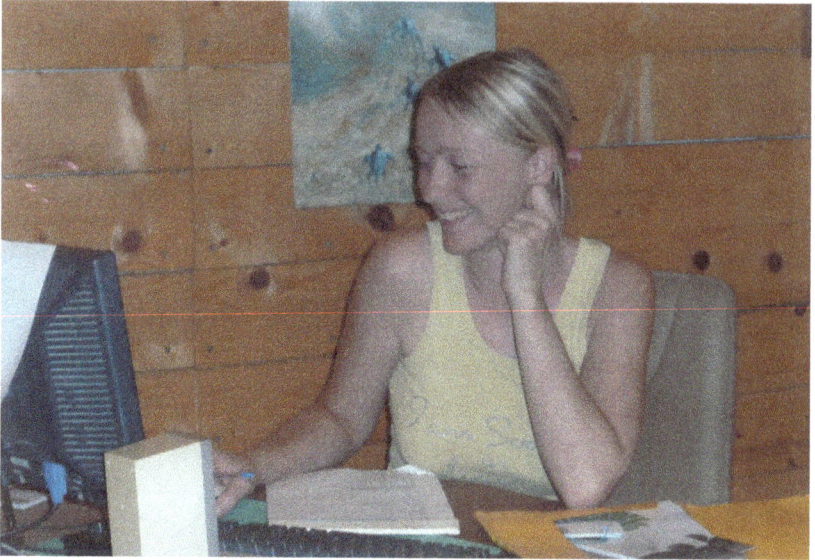

ABOVE, JONNA PEDERSEN, PROJECT MANAGER, REPLYING
TO DONATIONS ON LINE AT THE SANCTUARY, AND BELOW HER ASSISTANT,
EMILY MCLAUGHLIN, WHO IS STAYING WITH THE SANCTUARY THROUGHOUT
THE SUMMER. IT'S HARD, HOT WORK, BUT THEY ARE STILL SMILING.

TURTLES OF THE WORLD

There are seven different species of turtle on our planet, and the worrying thing is that they are all on the decrease. This should concern us all, as there are so many animals that are in danger of becoming extinct. This indeed is a worry; the climate change is a big problem, and its effects are catastrophic. Man, himself, has also played a part in decreasing the wildlife, with the destroying of the rainforests, etc., just for profit. The information which you will read next is of the turtles, all seven species. We start with the loggerhead.

THE LOGGERHEAD TURTLE

The Latin name for the loggerhead is *Caretta caretta*. The turtle has a large head; the carapace length in between 80 and 110 cm. The weight of the turtle is between 70 to 170 kilos. Hatchlings weigh about 20 grams. The colour of the turtle is a reddish-brown, it has a slightly heart-shaped top shell (carapace) with pale yellowish bottom shell (plastron). Hatchlings are brown to dark grey.

Global IUCN status

Endangered, population trend N/A.

Location

Found in the Mediterranean and Atlantic. Approximate population size nesting females: 60,000.

Diet

Omnivorous.

Food

Molluscs and crustaceans.

Habitat

Loggerheads occupy three different ecosystems during their lives: beaches (terrestrial zone), water (oceanic zone), and nearshore coastal areas.

Lifespan

The loggerhead can live up to about 80 years, but possibly more! Sexual maturity is between 20 and 30 years. Clutch size is around 100, but can be more.

Threats

Accidental capture in fishing gear, primarily in longlines and gillnets, but also in trawls, traps and pots, and dredges, directed harvest, not forgetting plastic bags, bottles, etc.

Fun Fact

The loggerhead has the largest and most powerful jaws of all the sea turtles in order to crush its prey. It is possible for them to take off a man's hand.

Other

The loggerhead carries more encrusting organisms like barnacles than other marine turtle species.

THE LEATHERBACK TURTLE

The Latin name for the leatherback is *Dermochelys coriacea*. The turtle has a thin layer of rubbery skin, strengthened by thousands of tiny bones. The carapace length is between 130 and 183 cm.

The weight of the leatherback is an amazing 300 to 500 kilos. Hatchlings weigh about 45 grams. The colour of the turtle is primarily a black shell with pinkish-white colouring on their belly.

Global IUCN status

Critically endangered, population trend, decreasing.

Location

The leatherback is found in the Pacific and Atlantic Ocean, approximate population size nesting females around 34,000.

Diet

Gelatinivores, their diet consists exclusively of jellies and other soft-bodied invertebrates like tunicates and sea squirts.

Food

Soft-bodied animals, such as jellyfish and salps and also pyrosomes.

Habitat

Leatherbacks are commonly known as pelagic (open ocean) animals, but they also forage in coastal waters.

Lifespan

The lifespan of a leatherback turtle is N/A. The sexual maturity of the leatherback is between 6 and 10 years, so it becomes sexually mature much earlier than the loggerhead turtle. The clutch size is also different, as it lays 80 eggs, so it lays the least, bar one, the least being the flatback.

Threats

They are harvested for the eggs and turtles themselves. Other threats include heavy rain and very high tides, which will flood the nests and drown the unhatched turtles, and of course the predators that lay in wait for the hatchlings as they head for the sea. This, of course, applies to all the different species of turtle, only one or two in 1000 are expected to reach maturity.

Fun Fact

The leatherback is the largest of all living sea turtles and also the deepest diver. Leatherbacks could swim alongside some of the deepest diving whales, they are capable of diving at a depth of at least 3900 feet!

Other

Genetically and biologically unique.

THE GREEN TURTLE

The Latin name for this turtle is *Chelonia ydas*. The meaning of this is the colour of fat under the shell. The carapace length is between 83 and 114 cm. The weight of the green turtle is around 110 to 190 kilos. The hatchlings weigh 25 grams. The top shell (carapace) is smooth with shades of black and grey, green, brown, and yellow, their bottom shell (plastron) is a yellowish-white.

Global IUCN Status

These turtles are endangered, and the population trend is decreasing.

Location

The green turtle is globally distributed and generally found in tropical and subtropical waters along continental coasts and islands between 30 north and 30 south. Nestings occurs in over 80 countries. The approximate population size of nesting females is 203,000.

Diet

Herbivorous.

Food

Seagrasses and algae.

Habitat

Beaches for nesting, open ocean convergence zones, coastal areas for 'benthic' feeding.

Lifespan

The green turtle's life span is N/A, sexual maturity is between 20 to 50 years, and is among the two top turtles to have such a long maturity time. The clutch size is 135 eggs

Threats

They are harvested for the eggs and meat (historically, though the practice continues in some areas of the world), incidental capture in fishing gear, and fibro papillomatosis, which is a disease.

Fun Fact

Green sea turtles are able to hold their breath for hours at a time. As they are cold-blooded, the colder the water, the longer they are able to hold their breath!

Other

Largest of all the hard-shelled sea turtles.

THE HAWKSBILL TURTLE

The Latin name, *Eretmochelys imbricata*, means 'narrow head and hawk-like beak'. The carapace length is from 71 to 89 cm. Their weight in kilos is in between 46 to 70 kilos, hatchlings weight is a mere 15 grams, making them the second lightest out of all the sea turtles. The top shell (carapace) is dark to golden brown, with streaks of orange, red, and/or black, with a serrated back and overlapping 'scutes', while the bottom shell (plastron) is clear yellow.

Global IUCN Status

Critically endangered, population trend decreasing.

Location

The hawksbill turtle is found in the Pacific and the Caribbean. The approximate population size of nesting females is a very worrying 8000 only.

Diet

Omnivorous.

Food

Sponges and other invertebrates, algae.

Habitat

Hawksbill turtles use different habitats at different stages of their life cycle, but are most commonly associated with healthy coral reefs, mainly in the Pacific and Caribbean.

Lifespan

N/A. Sexual maturity is between 20 to 40 years, and clutch size is 130 eggs.

Threats

Habitat loss of coral reef communities, and harvesting of their eggs and meat. Commercial exploitation, increased recreational and commercial use of nesting beaches in the Pacific, incidental capture in fishing gear.

Fun Fact

Due to their sponge diet, their flesh is harmful to humans, as sponges contain toxic chemicals, which accumulate in the animal's tissues. It's estimated that one turtle can consume over 1000 pounds of sponges per year!

Other

Their highly coloured and patterned shell is the sole source of commercial tortoiseshell. Numbers have declined by over 80 percent during the last century.

THE FLATBACK TURTLE

Its Latin name, *Natator depressa*, means 'very flat shell'. The carapace length is 99 cm, and their weight is 90 kilos. Hatchlings weigh 43 grams. The carapace is pale greyish-green in colour with the outer margins distinctly upturned.

Global IUCN Status

Data deficient, population trend N/A.

Location

The flatback has the smallest geographic range of the seven sea turtle species. Their distribution is restricted to tropical regions of the continental shelf and coastal waters of northern Australia, southern Indonesia, and southern Papua, New Guinea. They are usually found in waters less than 200 feet in depth. Approximate population size of nesting females is 20,000.

Diet

Omnivorous.

Food

Sea cucumbers, jellyfish, soft corals, shrimps, crabs, molluscs, fish and seaweed.

Habitat

These turtles prefer shallow, soft-bottomed seabed habitats that are far from reefs. They nest only in northern Australia, on beaches on small offshore islands.

Lifespan

N/A. Sexual maturity is between 7 to 50 years of age and the clutch size is between 50 to 70 eggs.

Threats

They are harvested for meat and eggs and captured in fishing gear. They suffer from the destruction of nesting beaches from coastal development, pollution, and destruction of feeding habitat (coral reefs). Also, nests are preyed upon by the sand monitor lizard and birds, including night herons and pelicans. In some areas, feral pigs consume almost all their nests.

Fun Fact

Flatbacks are preyed upon by saltwater crocodiles, the largest reptile on earth! So they do not have too much of an easy life.

Other

N/A.

THE OLIVE RIDLEY TURTLE

The Latin name, *Lepidochelys olivacea*, means 'olive-green shell'. The carapace length is between 62 and 70 cm, and its weight is

35 to 45 kilos. Hatchlings weigh 28 grams. They are olive/greyish-green (darker in the Atlantic than in the Pacific) with a heart-shaped top shell (carapace) and 5-9 pairs of coastal 'scutes' with one or two claws on their flippers. Hatchlings emerge mostly black with a greenish hue on their sides.

Global IUCN Status

Endangered, population trend decreasing.

Location

Olive ridleys are found mainly in tropical regions of the Pacific, Indian, and southern Atlantic oceans, spending much of their life in the open ocean, but may also inhabit continental shelf areas and venture into bays and estuaries. Arribadas occur in places such as Mexico, Nicaragua, Costa Rica, Panama, Australia, and also parts of Africa. Approximate population size of nesting females will be around 800,000.

Diet

Omnivorous.

Food

Algae, crustaceans, molluscs.

Habitat

They inhabit coastal areas, including bays and estuaries, mainly 'pelagic'.

Lifespan

N/A. Sexual maturity is 15 years, and clutch size is 100 eggs.

Threats

Major threats include degradation of nesting beaches, particularly in India. Many of their nesting beaches are being destroyed by coastal development and subsequent erosion. Other threats include the direct harvest of turtles' eggs for human consumption and the capture of turtles in commercial fishing gear.

Fun Fact

It's unknown why some turtles nest in arribadas and others are solitary nesters. The Olive Ridley can use both strategies during a single nesting season, nesting in both groups and alone!

Other

Slightly upturned shell edges.

THE KEMP RIDLEY TURTLE

The Latin name is *Lepidochelys kempii*, named after Richard Kemp who studied/discovered them. It has similar nesting habits to the Olive Ridley turtle. The carapace length is between 58 and 66 cm. Its weight is 32 to 49 kilos, and hatchlings weigh 14 grams, which is the lightest hatchling out of all seven sea turtles. The adult Kemp ridley has an oval carapace that is almost as wide as it is long and is usually olive-grey in colour.

Global IUCN Status

Critically endangered, population trend N/A.

Location

In the United States, these turtles are found in the Gulf of Mexico and along the Atlantic coast as far north as Nova Scotia. The primary nesting grounds in Mexico are at Rancho Nuevo, in the state of Tamaulipas, and in Texas along the Padre National seashore. A small number have also nested further north along the Texas coast. However, 95 percent of all nesting occurs in Mexico in the state of Tamaulipas. Approximate population size of nesting females is only 1000.

Diet

Carnivore; food consists of crabs, fish, jellyfish, shrimp, and a variety of molluscs.

Habitat

Adult females can be found migrating hundreds or thousands of kilometres between feeding habitats. Their mating areas and their preferred nesting beach is in Rancho Nuevo, Tamaulipas, Mexico. Adult males appear to be non-migratory, and stay mainly in coastal waters around Rancho Nuevo.

Lifespan

They can live for 50 years, and they reach sexual maturity at 12 years. Their clutch size is 110 eggs.

Threats

Slaughtered in the millions for their eggs, meat, skin, and shells, their already reduced populations still suffer from poaching and over-exploitation, as well as incidental capture in fishing gear and habitat loss and alteration.

Fun Fact

This is the only species that nests primarily during the day!

Other

Smallest marine turtle, nest only along a small stretch of coastline in the Gulf of Mexico.

I hope that this information about the seven species of sea turtles helps you to realise how endangered these animals are. Needless to say, if we ignore the plight of these creatures, they will one day come to an end, which will be a great loss to us and the wildlife of this planet.

Of course, there are many other breeds of turtle. These will be freshwater, such as the common snapping turtle, and the alligator snapping turtle, which live in lakes, rivers and streams, the common snapping turtle being the more aggressive. Both these turtles live in the southern coast of America and Mexico.

Getting back to the discarding of rubbish, there was a turtle not so long ago that suffered great distress simply from a plastic straw! This straw somehow managed to be sucked in to one of the turtle's nostrils, causing breathing problems. Luckily there were some people who spotted the turtle's undoubtable torture and managed to pull the straw out. This must have been very painful for the turtle, as the whole length of the straw – all but about an inch – was embedded. It took some time to remove the object and the distress was very visible, but, none the less, they finally removed it. These people were not vets and they did get criticism from a few people, which I think was uncalled for as they saved this turtle from a slow and painful death. What did it matter as long as they got the job done? I am certain that the turtle was pleased that somebody cared enough to try.

The initials 'IUCN', which was described in the information about the sea turtles, means International Union for Conservation of Nature, and all information about wildlife internationally will be fed to the International Union for Conservation of Nature.

Another incident was a young hatchling being trapped in a plastic cup which had been left on the beach, the cup laying on its side. The hatchling crawled into it and could not get back out again, leaving it confused. It seems a small thing, but that cup could have cost the young turtle's life, something so simple and yet a great danger to the turtles that have just hatched. We must give these animals the best chance of survival; after all, their lives are full of danger. Let's not make man one of them by leaving rubbish on the beach. It's so simple to throw it in a bin or even take it home with you. It's not going to hurt us, but it can have a devastating effect on the young hatchling. Let's help Yannis Vardakastanis to ensure their future!

These two incidents seem rather bizarre, but, none the less, it proves if nothing else that these things do happen, and only too often. We must be more vigilant in this matter. I have said before that my wife and I have picked up lots of rubbish on the beach and on the water, and it gives us a good feeling inside to know that we might be saving an animal's life!

It would be a very nice world indeed if everyone did their part. It does give you a good feeling and you will certainly get the turtles that are endangered by this rubbish their most thankful respect!

THE TURTLES MINEFIELD

We all know that the turtle carries the eggs to the nesting place, but have you ever thought who the real mother of the eggs are? A strange question, I know, but when the turtle has laid its eggs it then goes back into the sea. So who is the real mother?

If I was to say that the sun and the beach are the eggs' real mother, you might think me mad! This, however, is very true. For 60 days the eggs lay in the sand hopefully undisturbed, but if it was not for the beach and the sun, which sends its warm rays to incubate the eggs, they would not survive. Of course, the sand helps protect them against the dangers that lurk above as well. If the sun decided to not exist anymore, then we would all be in trouble that is certain, and of course the turtle eggs would not hatch and perish. Maybe a surreal thought but it does make a lot of sense.

On the beaches where you will find turtle nests, they are normally cordoned off with some sort of fencing to prevent bathers and people walking on the beach from getting too near to the nests, as some nests are not discovered for one reason or the other. Without the fencing it would prove very dangerous for the eggs. This is where the term 'minefield' comes in. People that were on the beach would be unaware of any eggs if they were not protected by the fencing, and would possibly walk over the nests. This in turn would of course make the eggs basically explode under your feet and you would never know! This, without doubt, would kill all the eggs that were laying in the nest. So it is vital that you take care if you know that the beach that you are on could possibly be a nursery to these turtle eggs. Walk near the water's edge, do not start banging parasols in the sand, certainly not at the back of the beach as this is more likely to be where the nests are. So in a word, just be careful.

The young hatchlings seem to be suffering more than usual this year (2015) from birds that prey on them as they try to advance to the water's edge after hatching. There is a system that seems to work in America, and that is preventing the hatchlings from coming out of their nests in the light of day, which seems to be happening a little more these days. It is a simple method, by covering the nests that are due to hatch that day with a black box. Then at night time, the box is removed so that the hatchlings can approach the water's edge more safely. A simple idea but effective. This could save hundreds from a grizzly end. Yannis Vardakastanis is thinking of adopting this method as a simple thing like a box could save many of the turtles of Zakynthos.

VOLUNTEERS EXPERIENCE AND VIEWS AT THE EARTH, SEA & SKY SANCTUARY

I have asked some of the volunteers if they could give a personal view of what they think of being a volunteer at the turtle sanctuary. They were only too keen to comment, and these are some of the comments that were passed on to me, and I would like to thank them all for giving a little time from their busy schedules.

Jim's experience at Earth, Sea & Sky

Why I decided to do it

I heard about Earth, Sea & Sky from a good friend of mine who took part in the volunteering program in 2014. I then looked into the goals of the organisation. After doing some research, I became intrigued by how fast the centre expanded, which shows that Earth, Sea & Sky are extremely determined.

As a civil engineer, I believe I could make a significant contribution to the organisation so I decided to volunteer in August 2015.

What have I been doing?

With only some basic knowledge of turtles when I started, I have gained a lot of in-depth information about turtles. One of the most shocking facts I learnt was that only one to two out of 1000 hatchlings could survive and mature. The extremely low rate makes me feel I should contribute a lot more to protect the turtles and the environment. After learning the comprehensive knowledge. I tried my best to educate the tourists so that they can understand the terrible situation this long-living sea creature is in.

One of the last pieces the centre is missing is a winter house for the rescued turtles. As I studied civil engineering at university, I make use of it and put my structural mechanics and creativity together to design the winter house. Technical drawings and a Google Sketch 3D model were created. These will help Earth, Sea & Sky to have a preliminary idea when they start planning.

Why do I think it's important?

I found that the most important thing, from working at Earth, Sea & Sky, is that they are the pioneer here in Zakynthos to help the turtles. Their vision is unique and they always put turtles in the highest priority. To make it possible, teaching tourists how they can be part of this campaign is the first thing we should do. There is only so much effort one person can put in to make a difference, everyone should give their helping hands. Therefore, education is the first and most important thing to do. Apart from that, I believe we can always find the harmonic balance which benefits everyone. This is not an easy step but by working closely with the experienced conservationists, the locals and the government, there will be a perfect solution. The number of turtles is a powerful indicator of how the environment has been damaged due to tourism and the lack of effective city planning. Saving turtles is to make people realise the importance of respecting the natural environment.

Who will I recommend to?

I definitely have learnt a great deal but this volunteering opportunity is not for everyone. If you believe you can make a difference no matter how hard the journey is and you have huge respect for the natural environment, you will do amazingly here.

Final words

The natural environment is the base from where we develop. The more we respect the environment, the better our future will be. In order to create a sustainable, technology-advanced future, we should always think carefully what consequences our decision will bring and the turtles are trying to tell us that we have to take action now!

Why I joined Earth, Sea & Sky

Turtles have always fascinated me, strong and tough on the outside but soft in the inside. Over the past two years I have taken great interest in preserving the oceans, focusing on plastic pollution and overfishing in the oceans. During the summer of 2015 I was incredibly busy with my college application, preparing for the ACT and an internship; I wanted to do something different. A few years ago I had come into contact with Earth, Sea & Sky through Sea Life. I was too young at the time, but applied two years later and was accepted as a volunteer. Although I have no intentions of pursuing a career in conservation, it is definitely something that I am passionate about and plan to support in any capacity I can.

My impressions of my time at ESS

There is a lot of passion and dedication behind this organization, which is infectious. Although I was dedicated before to the cause, the past two weeks have truly taken it to the next level. The same can also be said about sea turtles, I have always tried to accumulate a firm understanding of sea turtles, but during the past two weeks I learned more about sea turtles than the past 18 years of my life combined. The turtle crisis must be addressed immediately and the mindset of the general public must be changed, but luckily there are people like Yannis who, with the help of great and dedicated volunteers, can give turtles a voice. These conservationists are vital to preservation of earth and its beautiful and diverse nature.

Joshua Glueck, Germany/New York.

My experience at ESS has definitely changed my perspective of conservation. Everything is not what it appears to be. Many may not realise the work that has been put in as it has not been voiced. The work that they do here through educating the volunteers and tourists is the defining point of this organisation and it is a privilege to be able to have enlightened, if only a few tourists, on the efforts and sustainable aspects associated with sea turtle rescue.

My position as a volunteer for 17 weeks has changed throughout the course of the nesting and hatchling season, progressively becoming less practical and more office-based. The highlight for me was seeing a turtle nest, which to me is a priceless opportunity and something I didn't think I would get to see, as they are critically endangered in Greece.

Being here, I have gained business knowledge that would be useful to starting my own sanctuary one day. My favourite part of this experience has definitely been that I was given the opportunity to be a project leader and to have someone believe in me enough to think I am capable of doing the job, which I now have the confidence to say that I am capable.

This kind of work is a lifestyle choice that I decided to make. I have had one of the best experiences of my life here through meeting people from all over the world and being able to unite over a topic which we are all strongly connected to. It has been wonderful to meet like-minded people who bring with them different qualities and who all contributed with their ideas and specialised skills. I have enjoyed the communal living and seeing the relaxed atmosphere that comes with the Greek culture. I have made friends for life out here and would recommend this to all the animal lovers out there.

Anna Jones, England.

Experience on the beach 03/09/2015

It was early morning down on Gerakas Beach before the beach was open to the tourists. Yannis and I went down to collect data on the night's turtle activities. Already on the beach there were three tourists who were trampling over the nests at the back of the beach. They had deliberately gone behind the rope protecting the nests and were walking on top of them. Unfortunately, there was no National Marine Park guard or Archelon staff there present to enforce the regulations and stop them.

Next, there came three hatchlings from a nest at the far end of the beach.

These three tourists started using flash photography when they saw the hatchlings. The first two hatchlings made it to the sea reasonably unaffected but the third was disorientated and fell on its back and was unable to continue to the water at this point. The waves came in and it was near enough to the water's edge to be taken by the sea, which was lucky.

Yannis asked the tourists to stop with the flash photography. They apologised and stated that they had no idea that it would affect the hatchling in this way and that they were unaware of the beach regulations set out by the National Marine Park or that the beach had been closed on their entering.

To this statement, they were asked to then go and speak to the director of the NMPZ and he would enlighten them to the procedures of this beach. They apologised again but did not leave the beach and proceeded to take photos of hatchlings from another nest without flash. By now the beach was open to the tourists and there was light enough for them all to see the hatchlings. Altogether the 10 hatchlings made it to the sea, however the seagulls took them straight out the water and none of them survived past the first 100 metres.

The confusion from the flash combined with the seagulls gives a survival rate of zero, as seen that day, for any hatchling during daylight hours. These uniformed tourists were unaware that the disorientated hatchlings cannot swim and therefore drown due to flash photography. However, they are not to blame; if the NMPZ enforced regulations, patrols for the beach and accepted seagull monitoring practices, the hatchlings would have survived!

On the other beach that we visited there were also hatchling tracks. One of these was headed towards the restaurant nearest the beach a good 200 meters away. A very long way for a little turtle. The lights from the restaurant had distracted it and it was following this strong light source, normally we would have expected it to have become dehydrated and died from exhaustion. However, this hatchling had a strong survival instinct and eventually it did find its way to the sea. Unfortunately, this is a rare happy ending. This is an example of the negative impact of today's tourism on the loggerhead sea turtles of Zakynthos.

Anna Jones

It's so important to make tourists aware of the turtle nests and the use of flash photography, which can endanger their survival.

Anna Jones, who is a volunteer for the turtle sanctuary, is exactly right; tourists, at least a good few of them, do not know the all-important rules when visiting the beaches where the turtle nests are. It's not their fault, but a little education would prevent them from maybe standing on an unmarked nest or even laying on them as they sunbathe. The beaches cannot have 24-hour attention through the lack of funding. There are roped-off areas that hopefully protect the nests, but sometimes it's evident that people have walked over it anyway, and this could be destroying some of the eggs.

People need to be aware of the fact that the beaches have an opening and shutting time. This must be explained more clearly to the people that use the beaches. Notice boards that inform the tourists and also the local people would be an asset and they could be written in a number of languages. This would give them the simple advice that is needed to protect the nests. Marine Park did attempt to print some signs that were tied to fencing on Kalamaki beach, but the sign was only A4-sized and unfortunately they finally fell off.

People will respond to a sign if it is permanent and big enough to see.

Yannis Vardakastanis, on Gerakas beach, decided that he would inform tourists of the times that they are permitted on the beach, which was probably a help to Marine Park. He knows full well that he hasn't got any authority, but he just wanted to do the very best that he could for the turtle nests. Yannis cares so much for the preservation of the hatchlings so he wasn't too bothered about having authorisation or not. After all, it is the preservation that is most important and you cannot argue with that!

Anna Jones has told me that she would like to come back as a volunteer next year; this year she is doing a 17week stint. It is people like Anna that makes me feel very humble. She is an asset to the sanctuary and it is people like Anna that will make the preservation of wildlife successful. I would like to thank Anna Jones for the information that she gave to me and I wish her well for her future in the preservation of wildlife.

MY EXPERIENCE ON BANANA BEACH WITH YANNIS

This was very exciting for me. I have explained about the box system that Yannis said he was going to introduce. I did not realise though that he already had one up and running. Yannis took me to Banana beach where the box was set up. I did not know though that he had a hatchling in it. The hatchling had a problem with one of its flippers preventing it from being able to move properly. It would not have been able to swim either and would probably become a meal for a cruising seagull.

The method of the box is simple, although Yannis has designed an inner section of the box. This prevents the turtle from moving around too much if it digs its way out of the sand. The sand has to be very damp and warm, but not hot. The hatchling will survive very easily in the box without further damage, and can happily stay in the box for a few days. Under normal circumstances, when the turtles are fit and well, this method will help prevent loss, and the young turtles can be let out under the cover of darkness, which will give them more chance of survival. The box itself must be covered over with sand to keep the box at a safe temperature. This very simple idea can save many hatchlings from predators that wait for the young turtles that struggle to the water's edge once they have hatched.

On Banana beach, Yannis tells me that there are 23 nests below the sand; this is a good amount. The good thing about Banana beach is that there is a part of it that is not contaminated by either sunbeds or beach bars, there is nothing on this part of the beach. The sand is also a good factor, it seems to be softer than most other beaches in Zakynthos. This is good news; it gives the young turtle a good start on its long journey that awaits it. This was indeed an experience that I would not like to have slipped by me. Yannis always amazes me with his knowledge of the sea turtles; when you think that he has told you everything, he then produces more information for you. This is certainly true with the volunteers that have had the privilege to work with him, they all have said the same.

It is only too obvious to me that Yannis is an exceptional man. His volunteers tell me that they learn so much from this man, and they go back home, wherever they come from, knowing that their lives are richer from the learning. What is even nicer is the fact that Yannis Vardakastanis does not accept that he knows all there is to know and likes to learn from others, albeit from his volunteers or from professors of animal preservation. He just likes to keep learning so that he can help the wildlife even more. It says a lot from a man from a humble background who has so much passion.

A HATCHLING ON GERAKAS BEACH TRYING TO OVERCOME A FOOTPRINT

AN EXPERIENCE ON
KALAMAKI BEACH

It was about five o'clock in the afternoon on a Monday when I saw three Archelon volunteers heading towards a turtle's nest. The nest had already seen the exit of many hatchlings from the day before, but six of them had to be put back and buried under the sand for a while longer, but it was now time to release them once again.

This caused great interest with a number of tourists, and they approached carefully, near to where the nest was. The members of Archelon were being very careful as they swept the sand off the buried hatchlings. As the hatchlings emerged, it was very clear that the sun was making it difficult for the young turtles to take the correct path towards the sea. What happened next was amazing. The tourists, guided by Archelon, held their beach towels in such a way that they caused a shadow blocking the sun's glare. I, myself, found an old palm leaf that was lying dormant on the beach, and I also created a shadow, then we all followed the hatchlings that we had adopted and escorted them safely to the water's edge. One of the turtles had difficulty finding its way, but one of the Archelon team guided it to the safety of the water by smoothing the sand, then with the flat of his hand started to pat the sand gently. This apparently gives the same type of vibration that the sea makes when hitting the beach. It was fascinating to watch as this young turtle responded to the vibration and was soon on its journey in the sea. The tourists respected this by staying clear, yes, they did take photos, but with no flashes.

It was so gratifying to see people of different nations responding to the plight of the young turtles. It will probably be something that they will never forget, or even experience again; it brought smiles to people's faces as these creatures made their way to the sea. They probably realise that they, in a small way, helped a little, as the turtles make their vigorous journey that lies in wait for them. We wish them the best of luck, and let's hope that in 20 or 30 years' time these young turtles return as adults to lay their own eggs on the beach of Kalamaki. My only concern is that maybe these hatchlings would have been even more safe if they were released a little later in the evening when darkness was arriving, and they would have a better chance of not becoming a meal for the predators that prowl in the light of day.

NEWS UPDATE

Latest research, led by Professor Brendon Goddey, has discovered all plastic that enters the sea is mostly still there, forming a soup of microplastics. This could have frightening repercussions causing danger to all seven species of sea turtle and other sea life. Manufacturers don't tell us to dump plastic, we do that ourselves! So the simple rule is make sure that all plastics, no matter in what shape or form it is, put it in its proper place, and let's prevent this disaster from getting any worse.

This year – 2015 – has seen a drop in the amount of successful hatchings. The drop is about 30%. Marine Park has had a loss of about 286 nests. This of course creates great concern. Gerakas beach nestings have been very successful, almost 100%; this is about 20% up on last year's count, and I think that it is because Marine Life introduced a simple rope barrier that kept tourists from straying onto the nests.

However, the nests on Sekania beach have a different story, some of the laying turtles buried their eggs too near the water's edge and because of that the sea has claimed the eggs, stopping them from developing into hatchlings. This of course is something that none of us can prevent, and although very sad, it's the wrath of nature.

The box that I have recently spoken about, that Yannis Vardakastanis introduced, is really working. About 80% of the hatchlings that are kept there survive. From about 8pm to 7am, the turtles, once in the sea, need the cloak of darkness to avoid predators, and as this gives them 11 hours to get into deeper waters, the young turtle will only swim close to the surface and will come up for air from time to time, but the journey could take 48 hours before they are completely safe.

When the hatchlings reach the water's edge, they will swim for about two and a half miles heading north east, then they will turn direction and head south simply out of instinct. The box that Yannis introduced should only be used when the turtles find it difficult to reach the sea and become exhausted, this will probably mean about 30%. When they are put into the box the sand must be moist and warm as I have said before and they will go back to sleep and regain their strength, giving them another chance the next day.

THE PICTURE ABOVE IS OF ANNA JONES WORKING HARD AT HER DESK. A VOLUNTEER THIS YEAR, SHE IS HOPING TO COME BACK NEXT YEAR AS ASSISTANT PROJECTS MANAGER. GOOD LUCK TO HER, AND OF COURSE HER FUTURE IN CONSERVATION.

Just recently there has been a slump in the amount of plastic bags sold in supermarkets in Scotland, as they are now charging a price of five pence per bag. The drop was a dramatic 80%. If this was introduced all around the globe just imagine the effect it would have on the problem of the plastic waste that we have at the moment. There is no real need to have a plastic bag every time we go into a supermarket or any other shop for that matter.

I know that in these modern times of ours we think that we should be presented with a bag when we shop. It is often said by the younger set mostly that the older generation did nothing for the environment. This, however, is certainly not in the least true.

When I was much younger, in the '50s and '60s, mostly in the '50s, we did more for the environment than today. We did not have plastic bags, but paper ones, which we sometimes used again for shopping. My mother and others would fold these bags neatly and put them to one side for the purpose of reusing. They also used them for wrapping parcels; most of the bags never had any advertising written on them, so they would save the expense of having to buy brown paper, but more importantly this would save more trees from being chopped down, something that is very important for our survival!

Plastic throwaway lighters did not exist, instead normal petrol lighters were used and when empty they would be filled again, so there was no plastic waste there either, more than can be said for today.

Bottles were all made of glass. These bottles, whether milk bottles or lemonade bottles, were delivered to the door, but they were collected every day by the milkman, or the lemonade man. The lemonade bottles had tops which had a wiring system which was threaded through the top of the bottle so when you opened the top, the top would not come away from the bottle. The lemonade bottles had a deposit on them, which was returned to you when the bottles were collected, or you would pay a lesser amount for new supply of lemonade. This is something I feel should be reintroduced, although there are some bottles that still have this system, but more importantly, there was no plastic being discarded left, right and centre. So all bottles were recycled.

In these days I speak of, there were not so many electrical appliances, so the use of electricity was no way near as much as today. Once again, this helped the environment from using an incredible amount of electricity, more than can be said today.

Petrol consumption was by far less. People either used buses or trains, or dare I say it, walked! Today most people use a car, even if they only have to travel 100 yards! The amount of pollution that is pumped out these days is very frightening. Yes, there are car manufacturers that work hard to cut this problem down, but they cannot compete with what we call the good old days. Maybe we all could start to cycle, a much better healthier method of transport. And we could certainly keep the planet healthier.

THE TROUBLE WITH PLASTIC

We cannot blame plastic itself, but the people that use it. It's only people that discard the plastic items. We cannot blame the factories that make them; as I have said before, they don't tell us to throw the rubbish all around the countryside, no, we decide to do that ourselves. We have recycling bins, let's use them. There are people that follow this code, and they should feel good about themselves for doing this simple thing, but alas there are many that do not seem to care.

I have seen only too often plastic items being thrown out of cars as they drive, leaving the now discarded bottles or bags and even paper items, not to mention tin cans, to roam freely around the countryside, finding a resting place as they bounce along the tarmac! It does not seem to matter, though, for these thoughtless few that want to turn their environment into a tip that would put a rubbish tip to shame.

This year I have noticed the rubbish that is spread around the olive groves to be more than common. Tourists notice as they take a photo.

The island of Zakynthos, where I live now, has this problem. It is a beautiful island, and these few thoughtless people who think nothing of their own island where they were born seem to think that it is their right to do whatever they like, and if it means turning their island into a rubbish dump, so be it!

I cannot understand this way of thinking; surely they understand if they continue to carry on infecting their island this way somewhere along the line tourists will react by not coming over for their holidays. This of course will affect the island's economy. Maybe then these selfish people will then become aware when their jobs become extinct! If we all just do our bit, we won't have any problems. To take your rubbish home is not impossible, the wildlife will gain from this small task as well.

I think that we need to take a closer look of how we did things in the past. I think that we could all learn a new lesson from the old ones!

THE PICTURE ABOVE IS OF ONE OF THE MEADOWS IN GERAKAS.

Luke Durkin—Bicester, Oxfordshire, England

Earth, Sea & Sky Volunteer 27/06/15-18/07/15

My experience at Earth, Sea & Sky (ESS) is something I will certainly never forget. ESS is a triumph in many ways, I have to admire how Yannis has taken his own personal passion for sea turtles and turned it into a thriving volunteering network and information centre. The scale of his passion cannot be underestimated, during the nesting season he is at Gerakas beach before 7am every day, dragging some of us volunteers to help him survey the beach. Despite the early rise, I was always keen to do the morning survey, to see the action being taken to ensure the survival of the loggerhead hatchlings and to see Yannis' personal battle against the almost useless National Marine Park (NMP). Almost every survey I was part of, NMP and ARCHELON (the other sea turtle conservation group on the island) would consistently miss turtle nests, leaving them unmarked and vulnerable to the onslaught of tourists.

Another enlightening experience was the night survey. Seeing the dazzling lights of Laganas and the illegally built buildings encroaching onto the nesting beaches, really hit home the importance of ESS informing the public on what has to be done to protect the endangered loggerheads. I couldn't quite believe what had once been one of the largest loggerhead nesting bays had been so devastated by tourism and that almost none of the Greek people seemed to care.

Day to day at the centre, work never seemed to stop. Jonna, the ever-enthusiastic project manager at ESS, made sure that every day that all the volunteers had something to do. Despite the centre being quiet at times, we were always engaged in something to do with ESS, something either to keep the centre going or looking at ways to improve. The centre in itself is really quite impressive, it has all of the qualities to be an excellent sea turtle rescue centre. However, it has been like this since 2012 and has not held a single sea turtle, even though it has the facilities to do so. This needs to change. So I was so glad that Jonna and Yannis had the same drive for change.

As a group, the other volunteers and I were given responsibility to try to look for ways to gain the finances needed to expand ESS and to open the much-needed clinic for the injured sea turtles. I was so impressed with how everyone took on the tasks set in front of them with such enthusiasm, and I couldn't help but think this is because how ESS treat us volunteers. I was treated excellently over my time at ESS and I was more than happy to help them in any way could, even after I had left the volunteering programme.

For the future, I think ESS need to concentrate on opening the clinic as it is such as massive project that needs to be up and running as soon as possible. I have no doubt that all the staff, interns and volunteers at ESS will build a larger, more effective community in the coming years, which will support the loggerhead sea turtle conservation on the island. But all in all, I cannot fault my experience and would recommend anyone enthusiastic in animal conservation to consider joining the ESS volunteer programme or even just donating to their cause.

Upon arrival at the 'turtle rescue centre' in Glyfada, Athens, it is difficult to differentiate between what is a decrepit worksite foreman's office and what is the entrance, which doesn't bode well for a first impression. Gingerly we entered the centre which is poorly laid out and proceeded to enter the so-called information building which is a small shed-like room you need to pass through to make your way to the recovery/winter house, with a single volunteer manning this room, who although friendly enough he clearly lacked basic knowledge. He frequently simply said 'I don't know' to many questions, which is a reflection on the training or moreover the lack of it that is given to those who work there. Moving into the recovery/winter house was a huge shock and not a positive one, the only way to describe it would be to call it a plastic-covered greenhouse full of black plastic buckets. The room is clearly not a suitable place to house an injured animal for a prolonged period of time as the facilities are simply less than basic. Although, yes, it is important for an injured turtle to be kept in a small environment upon first arriving with an injury. It is also vital that they are not kept in it beyond the required recovery time. The room was filled with 20 of these plastic buckets, each containing a single turtle, many of whom are distressed and agitated at how long they have been confined for and their solution is to simply cover the turtle's container with tarpaulin. When talking to the manager with regards to the turtles' recovery he was very evasive and didn't seem willing to answer the questions posed to him. What stands out the most about his replies was he claimed that once the turtles are fully recovered, they then test their diving to see if they are ready to be released back into the wild. However, this is quite frankly a delusion or a deliberate lie as there is simply no possible way to do this with the facilities they have there. Which could quite possibly explain why they have had a turtle there for three years, which to me is pure torture for that poor turtle who by now has been in captivity too long to survive back in the wild so is now confined to live out his life with very little stimulation. While there I also witnessed how they record the temperature of each turtle container and it was quite frankly a joke. One person went round to each container putting a thermometer into the water for all of 2 seconds then recording it and moving on. This clearly has no standing as a result as it is impossible for a thermometer to record a temperature within that time frame. However bad my opinion of all of this had been, I was then informed of how their filter system works and it is completely unacceptable, as they do not have any filters for any of the tanks they use. They simply drain water in and out from the nearby sea, this may not seem like something that bad until you realise that everything from faeces to antibiotics and cleaning products is sent out into the ocean and pollutes the sea around the local area. This is going to have an impact on all life forms nearby and I believe that if you are going to be a conservationist then you must think of all areas not just the area you are working on as it is very contradictory. Having said all this, I believe the idea they have in trying to help and conserve the turtles of Greece is very noble and important. They simply do not do that with the current centre they are operating from as it is just not up to the job and given how long they have been operating for, if we leave the fate of the turtle in the hands of these people, then there will be no hope of a future for these ancient creatures.

Jordan Walsh

The information that Anna and Jordon came back with from Glyfada near Athens from the turtle sanctuary does not make impressive reading. This is why it is so important that the sanctuary in Zakynthos becomes an important place for the turtles that are injured or weak hatchlings that need to be made stronger for their journey ahead.

Recently, though, Yannis and Jonna had a meeting set up with Marine Park's president so that they could present their proposals for improved protection methods on Gerakas beach. The meeting was set for the 29/10/15. Unbeknown to Yannis and Jonna, the meeting was cancelled, but Marine Life failed to inform them both and they only discovered this on their arrival. I do not understand Marine Life's methods in Zakynthos. Here they have a perfect opportunity to get other organisations involved, such as Earth, Sea & Sky's sanctuary, but seem very shy of the fact that these people can really help and have offered their help in the past without result.

The good news was that Marine Life did see them the day after and listened to some of their proposals. It is expected to take a little time to get answers back from Marine Life. I hope that the outcome will be very favourable to all those involved.

SOME VERY WORRYING NEWS ON ONE OF THE WORLDS FAVOURITE ANIMALS

In Indonesia, the orangutans living in the forests have become the victims of the greedy. This greed caused by illegal logging and land-clearing for the sake of the palm oil industry has destroyed the most rich and biodiverse rainforests. Every hour there is the equivalent of 300 football fields of forest destroyed. This is to make way for the palm oil plantations that are ever growing at such a rate that they have destroyed three quarters of all the forests that the orangutan need to survive. The way they clear the forests are with fire and logging. Just recently there have been orangutans burnt to death, leaving some of the young without parents. Some orangutans have escaped death, but have been burnt so badly that they might not live, or they may become maimed for life. This is not an option, the murdering and maiming of these animals for profit and without any remorse is nothing short of disgusting.

In the last two decades, 3.5 million hectares of forest has been destroyed. Around 80% of orangutan habitat has been wiped out by this greed for money, thus 6000 orangutans have been lost! Elephants and tigers have also fell victim, there are only 400 Sumatran tigers left. Palm oil is found in over half of all packaged items on the shelves of supermarkets.

Let's get this straight, if we allow these greedy companies to continue with this then there will be not enough trees to support life for the animals that live there. Also I think that maybe they should think less about money and start thinking about the human race! We ourselves depend on the oxygen that comes from trees to survive too! So let's stop this stupidity. While we allow these greedy, rich, selfish people to continue with their destruction of the planet, they will indeed carry on with their careless killing of all the animals that rely on the forests. It's about time that we woke up and put a stop to this insane self-destruction. If not, then we all deserve to let these greedy industries get richer and watch as the world falls into decay!

AN IN-DEPTH DESCRIPTION OF THE LOGGERHEAD TURTLE

The loggerhead sea turtle is the world's second largest hard-shelled turtle. Adults have an average weight ranging from about 80 to 200kg, and a length range of about 70 to 95cm. The biggest turtle ever reported was an amazing 545kg.The biggest carapace length reported was 213 cm.The underside shell is, as I have said, called the plastron.

The carapace is divided into large plates, or scutes. Twelve pairs of scutes rim the carapace, and five vertebral scutes run down the shell's midline, while a further five pairs of costal scutes boarder them. The nuchal scute is found at the base of the turtle's head. There are a further three pairs of inframarginal scutes which form the bridge of the shell.

The shell, of course, serves as an armour, but of course the turtle cannot retract their heads or their flippers into the shell, so they can be subject to attacks from larger sea creatures such as sharks and seals, which can be evident by the scars, or even chunks that have been taken from them.

The loggerhead belongs to the family Cheloniidae, and is found in the Atlantic, Pacific and Indian oceans, and of course the Mediterranean Sea. The turtle will spend most of its life in saltwater and estuarine habitats. Females are the only ones that will come ashore. In the nesting season they will lay an average of four clutches of eggs. Then they produce no more eggs for about two to three years.

The loggerhead turtle is omnivorous, feeding on bottom-dwelling invertebrates. It has very powerful jaws which serve as very effective tools, and can easily crush and rip its prey.

Male loggerheads have longer tails and claws than the female. The claws are used to hang on to the female as they mate and normally leave scars on the female's shell. The female's shell is more domed than the male, which has a flatter carapace. Males also have a wider head than the female also.

The sex of the turtle cannot be determined when it is juvenile or subadult through external anatomy, only by dissection can the sex be made evident.

The loggerhead has lachrymal glands which are located behind each eye, this allows the turtle to maintain osmotic balance by eliminating excess salt which is obtained from ingesting sea water. When on land this gives the impression that the turtle is crying.

The largest concentration of the loggerhead is found along the south eastern coast of North America and the Gulf of Mexico. Florida is the most abundant for nesting sites with an amazing 67,000 or more nests, but when you think that only one or two survive out of every 1000 eggs, there could be as little as 134 that reach maturity.

The largest Indian Ocean nesting site is Oman on the Arabian Peninsula. Nestings can be around 15,000; this makes it the second largest nesting ground in the world, but once again only one or two will survive from every 1000, making it as little as 15 to 30 that will once again reach maturity.

Western Australia plays a part as well, with 1000 to 2000 nests. No need to tell you the survival rate that is expected here.

Greece is the most popular nesting area in the Mediterranean with about 3000 nests, Zakynthos being the more popular area, which probably is home to more than half the 3000. Zakynthos authorities do not allow planes to take off at night as the planes can play a part in the disturbance of the nests. Cyprus and Turkey also accommodate nesting sites. The Mediterranean Sea is a nursery for young turtles as well as the adults. This is very true in spring and the summer months. Nearly half of the Mediterranean juvenile population has migrated from the Atlantic.

Loggerheads spend most of their lives in the ocean and shallow coastal waters, where they live in a floating mat of sargassum algae. This is where they find an abundance of food which they share with other creatures of the sea. A possible one hundred species of animals which also live in the sargassum becomes food for the turtle. Ants, flies, aphids, beetles are carried by the wind and end up on the sargassum which gives the turtles part of a very healthy diet.

Loggerheads are more active in the course of the day; they spend about 85% of their day submerged. The males are more active than the females and will dive more often. The average diving time is between 15 and 30 minutes, but they can stay submerged up to an amazing four hours!

When the turtles decide to rest they spread their forelimbs to about mid-stroke swimming position, they then remain motionless with their eyes half-open and are easily alerted. Captives will sleep in the same position but their eyes are tightly closed, as they probably haven't got so much to worry about!

Water temperature affects the turtles' metabolic rate, when the temperature drops to around 13 and 15 centigrade, they will become lethargic. The loggerhead will take a floating cold-stunned posture. Younger turtles have more resistance to the cold waters and do not become stunned until the temperature drops below nine centigrade.

In England not so long ago there were two loggerhead turtles spotted by walkers along the Dorset coast near Swanage. They would be in grave danger as the waters would be well below safe temperatures. Feeding would be a problem as when the water is too cold, they will not feed. The Marine Conservation Society (MCS) were informed. There were concerns that the turtles would become hypothermic; this would indeed be dangerous to the turtles. If the turtles were still alive, and were rescued they would not be able to put them back in the sea, this would be a death sentence to them both. Let's hope that all will be well with them and they carry on living their lives to the full. I wish them all the luck in the world.

Female-female aggression, which is rare in other marine vertebrates, is common with the loggerheads. Ritualised aggression can go from just threat displays to actual combat. Normally this will be over feeding grounds. They will snap at each other's jaws, which could inflict serious damage. They will either mutually stop, or one chases the other off from the feeding ground.

The loggerhead turtle seems to be territorial and will fight with loggerheads and turtles of different species.

The loggerhead has a greater list of known prey than any other sea turtle. Food items include sponges, corals, sea anemones, barnacles, sea urchins, sea cucumbers, star fish and jellyfish.

The amount of predators that the loggerhead turtle has is startling. They have to run the gauntlet as soon as they hatch, trying to make it to the sea before they get eaten. The dangers also lie when they are eggs. The eggs are attacked by ants, beetles, fly larvae, also snakes contribute to the turtle eggs demise, as well as the red fox. This is true in Australia, where they are only too regular and can wipe out a whole nest. Of course, there are many more predators that make their claim to the unfortunate eggs that lie helplessly beneath the sands, but thankfully there is a healthy amount that do survive their enemies. When you consider the amount of predators that do destroy the nests, when they are trying to reach the sea, and not forgetting the predators beneath the sea such as ghost crabs and fish that also like to have young turtle on the menu, they have a pretty rough time in their survival. The raccoon, however, is the most destructive, leaving nothing in the nest alive, it is almost 100% of everything they dig up. Not very good news for the future of these condemned eggs!

Parasites and also disease will attack hatchlings and eggs. Fibro papillomatosis disease is caused by a form of the herpes-type virus which can give the turtle internal and external tumours. These tumours can affect essential behaviours; if the eyes are affected it can cause blindness that will become permanent.

It is incredible that there are over 100 species of life that lives on the turtle, which would include about 13 phyla and 37 different kinds of algae. None of these are of any benefit to the loggerhead and can cause drag as it swims, but the shell discolouration can help the turtle to be more camouflaged.

Incubation lasts for about 80 days. The hatchlings will then dig through the sand and reach the surface. This usually occurs in the hours of darkness, which increases their chances of escaping the predators that lie in wait for them, and of course from the sun's hot rays that beat onto the sand which can burn the turtle as it tries to make it to the sea. The hatchlings find the ocean by following the bright reflections from the moon and the light of the stars that reflect on the water's surface. Once in the water they will swim nonstop for about 20 hours or more.

Carolus Linnaeus gave the turtle its first binomial name, *Testudo caretta*, in 1758. Over the next two centuries 35 names emerged, this led to the name *Caretta caretta*, which was introduced in 1902 by Leonhard Stejneger. The loggerhead, the English common name, refers to the turtle's large head. The loggerhead belongs to the family Cheloniidae, this includes all sea turtles except one, which is the leather back sea turtle. The loggerhead turtle has been around for millions of years, out-living all the other animals that roamed so long ago. Loggerhead turtles vary in size; Mediterranean loggerheads are smaller than the ones that live in the Atlantic, both are descended from colonising loggerheads from Tonga Land, South Africa.

The sexes of the loggerhead are determined by the temperature of the sand that they are nesting in. Higher temperatures may make ratios more in favour for the female. If the temperature is around 30 centigrade, this may lead to an even amount in both.

The female turtle will mate with as many as five males for one nest, this explains the differences in colouration in the hatchlings, some are more of a lighter brown, and others are very dark. In the nest itself, the eggs that are more in the middle of the clutch will more than likely to be larger than the others when they hatch.

THE FACTS THAT WILL CAUSE
· RACING EXTINCTION

Every year America throws away 254 tonnes of garbage, so imagine how much rubbish worldwide that is discarded. It's not very promising for the future for everything that lives on this planet of ours, including us. Seeing that we are the only contributors, and can only blames ourselves for discarding rubbish, I think that we owe this planet an apology. The animals don't go round creating mountains of rubbish, we do! It is the wildlife that is affected almost to extinction. Is that fair? I think not. Let us all do something positive and decrease the mess and of course the certain demise of this planet.

Plastic is killing our sea life; 270,000 tonnes of plastic pollute our oceans every year. Every year animals die in their thousands because of this.

Landfills in America make them the third largest source of methane.

Reusable bags need to be introduced, instead of the plastic bag that is only too commonly used at a terrifying rate. Plastic bags take about 1000 years for them to rot.

There are five countries that cause the most pollution; Europe, India, Russia, China and America. It's plainly evident that these countries need to make drastic changes. Without them, well, time's running out!

One in six species of animal life will become extinct if we do not lower greenhouse gases; we could be one of them! This is our last chance to put things right, to curb climate change. If not, half of the wildlife on this planet will become extinct in 100 years' time.

Since 1999, more than 39,000 African animals have become trophies and have been legally shipped through Seattle.

TAP Air, an airline from Portugal, have ended the shipment of animals that are destined for use in experiments and body parts of endangered animals. This is a great credit to them.

We must get every shipment source to refuse delivery of animals that are experimented on. Only then can this disgusting industry become extinct and not the animals.

I would suggest that if this is so important to them, let the people that are happy to see this happen become the experimented upon! Leave these poor animals that have to suffer horrendous pain just so that they can make a profit.

Stop killing sharks just for their fins. Most times, the shark has to suffer having its fin cut off while still alive and thrown back into the oceans to die horrifically. Hunting manta rays in Indonesia must be stopped. FEDEX, the parcel carriers, has a choice to make. Are they going to join UPS and other shipping companies and refuse to deliver? The choice is very simple.

SITTING AT A MEETING WITH SEA LIFE

Visiting Yannis just recently I had the pleasure of meeting two people who are members of Sea Life. Andy Bool ,who is head of Sea Life Trust, and Mark Oakley, who is head of PR for Sea Life. They had come over to Zakynthos to visit Yannis and hopefully offer their support for the sanctuary. Mark, who has, I believe, visited Yannis several times throughout the years as a friend and also a means for helping Yannis to get the sanctuary to become an important part for the preservation of the turtles and the wildlife on Zakynthos. Mark is a keen birdwatcher, like myself, I am pleased to say. Andy was a pleasure to meet, and this was his first visit to Zakynthos and the sanctuary and he was very impressed at what he had seen here. He will be a big asset to Yannis in the future no doubt. He knows that there are a lot of things to be done to make the sanctuary even more of a success.

The reason for the meeting with Yannis and Jonna was to talk things out, and what had precedence. There were a lot of things to talk about, way above my head. I did not realise there was so much involved. The word 'money' always shows its evil head, but it is needed to get the sanctuary to move forward. You must remember the sanctuary is an NGO, and Yannis has to raise this money, with a little help of course, but mostly by himself.

Sea Life, I'm certain, will do all they can to support him, but even they cannot do everything. I was pleased that they let me sit in on their meeting and I learned a lot from it. I certainly learned some of the politics that are involved. The meeting went on for two or more hours, but was far from boring. Ideas from everyone were being suggested; even I had a small say in the matters that were talked about. I became very interested in how these people want to preserve wildlife. These sorts of people are a tremendous help to our planet; the dedication is shown with every word they speak. Mark and Andy seem to work tirelessly, the optimism that these people have is commendable. The knowledge they have made me feel like I knew nothing! Which I suppose is true. I have learned a lot, or at least I think so, but when it comes to these two people, I realise that I really know next to nothing.

I was so pleased, though, sitting with all four people at the meeting – I exclude myself of course – listening to everyone and the depth of that conservation was truly an eye opener. I wish everyone well with the plights that they have to deal with on a daily basis. Saving the wildlife everywhere in the world is no mean feat. I wish that everybody was as dedicated as these four people; the planet would not have any worries whatsoever.

I hope that everything they have spoken about will become a fact one day soon. The sanctuary is unique and needs to be supported. If reading this helps you also to want to support the turtle sanctuary then by all means do so. This sanctuary that Yannis has built throughout the years deserves support. Mark and Andy will be traveling to Glyfada in the mainland of Greece to see for themselves what kind of sanctuary they have to host the injured turtles. I think that what they will see will sadden them and make them realise what the sanctuary of Zakynthos can do for the turtles' survival. I wish them both well for now and the future and look forward to meeting them again soon.

I would like to give a personal big thank you to both of you, Yannis and Jonna, for allowing me to attend the meeting with you all. Best regards, Michael James Elves.

I first met Yannis more than 20 years ago at the Scarborough Sea Life Centre when he and Anna (his wife back then) came to meet us to see if we could provide a permanent home for three injured turtles languishing in the rescue centre at Glyfada (Athens).

They had recently visited the Athens facility and been moved by the plight of three loggerheads too badly injured ever to resume life in the wild.

Fotini, the saddest of the three, had no front flippers. Lefteris was missing one front and one rear flipper. And the third casualty, Antiopi, was recovering from a gaping head wound which had left her brain damaged.

They were all in small circular bins in shallow water, taking up space that was urgently needed for new arrivals. Unless they could be rehomed they would probably have had to be euthanised.

Of course we offered them a home, which delighted Anna and drew a warm smile from Yannis, who seemed in that first meeting to be a shy and enigmatic character, happy to stay in the background.

Almost as a parting gesture, he casually dropped a few leaflets and brochures on the table, some of them promoting the holiday property rentals that he and Anna offered in and around Gerakas.

I had been to Zakynthos two or three times, to the village of Kypselli in the north, and I was already hooked on the jewel of the Ionian. Yannis and Anna seemed to be offering something different, however, something a lot less commercial and much closer to nature.

I couldn't resist. Thus began an annual pilgrimage that saw my family and I quickly fall in love with Gerakas. We returned so often that Yannis effectively saw my daughter grow up.

We were beguiled, as so many have been, by his passion for the wildlife of his island and his determination to save as much as can be saved from the ravages of the tourism industry. Seeing those ravages had sharpened Yannis' appreciation of the natural world he was privileged to grow up in, and he has the true philosopher's gift of being able to impart a measure of that appreciation to all who hear him talk on the subject.

That was how he persuaded my daughter, Jennifer, and I to devote a full day of our first Gerakas holiday to collecting discarded fishing nets, plastic and other human debris from several of the local beaches.

Over time, Yannis became a very close friend. A little over 10 years ago he suggested that Sea Life centres — for whom I have handled public relations for nearly quarter of a century now — help him raise the funds to build a turtle rescue centre at Gerakas.

If we could turn back the clock, I don't think either of us would entertain such an ambitious challenge again. Lots of money was indeed raised and there is a fabulous facility in Gerakas to show for it... But the hurdles along the way almost bankrupted Yannis, and there are bureaucratic hurdles still to negotiate before rescue work can actually commence. It does, however, already provide a fitting base for Earth, Sea & Sky's invaluable nest protection work and raising awareness of the ever-deteriorating prospects of the island's loggerhead turtles.

My family and I have seen first-hand how Yannis' uncompromising efforts on behalf of the turtles have at times placed him at odds with neighbours, other villagers, local officialdom, other conservation groups and even his own family. My wife looks upon Yannis almost like a prodigal son, and at times has been quite concerned about his psychological well-being given the forces ranked against him.

His many struggles have taken their toll for sure. There is a little less vigour and a hint of battle weariness in his demeanour, but no less determination.

While others seek a diplomatic course to achieving the many protective measures needed to ensure the long-term survival of the Zakynthos turtles, Yannis knows there just isn't time. He will continue to point out the gross insufficiency of current measures no matter who it upsets, and continue to do what he can to directly safeguard as many nests as he can without landing himself in jail, in the hope that the message gets through before it is too late.

Those three disabled turtles at Glyfada did eventually move to the UK.

A thorough veterinary check-up and x-rays on arrival revealed that Fotini was suffering from a painful degenerative bone disease, and it was clear to all involved that the only humane option for her was to put her out of her misery, which was done swiftly and painlessly.

Lefteris enjoyed a further 10 years swimming around the ocean tank at Scarborough until finally succumbing to complications arising from his original injuries.

Antiopi is still alive and healthy, though her behaviour is still of course a little erratic because of the brain injury she sustained. She has become a great ambassador for her species, quietly and unwittingly raising awareness of the work that Yannis and others like him are doing around the world to try and save one of the ocean's most iconic creatures.

I would like to thank Mark Oakley for taking time out to write his comments on Yannis Vardakastanis and what he is trying to do for the wildlife of Zakynthos.

THE PLIGHT OF THE OLIVE RIDLEY IN COSTA RICA

This is a recent event in Costa Rica. The Olive Ridley sea turtle that nests on the beaches of Costa Rica found a nightmare waiting for them as they reached the beach to nest. There were hundreds of the turtles trying to move along the beach to lay their eggs, only to be confronted with hordes of tourists that seem to run amok when sighting the unfortunate animals. The tourists stood in the turtles' path as they attempted to move over the sandy beach. They also took photographs using the flash on their cameras! This is something that you never do, but they did it anyway. The adults even stood the children on the turtles just for the sake of a photo for the holiday album. They must have known this would be stressful for the turtle, or were they that blind to being sensible.

The beach has been protected since 1982, and there were only two guards monitoring a four-mile beach! They could not cope with the hordes of tourists that were trampling around the turtles, it was like a human frenzy, almost treading on them just for the sake of looking.

These turtle eggs are allowed to be harvested in Costa Rica, so there are thousands of eggs that do not stand a chance of swimming in the oceans. The turtles, most of them anyway, returned to the safety of the sea, but also released their eggs into the waters. The eggs would not survive, so due to human stupidity, Costa Rica lost thousands of eggs, not very good for the future of the turtle. There were turtles that did lay their eggs, but with a crowd of onlookers that surrounded them. What a terrible disaster! People everywhere in the world must start to learn that they cannot just do as they like with any creature in the wild so that they can have a photo to take back home with them when their holiday is over.

If they carry on like the tourists in Costa Rica, then in years to come that is the only thing that will be left to look at – a photo!

YANNIS VARDAKASTANIS AND HIS PERSONAL THOUGHTS ON HIS BEAUTIFUL ISLAND, AND WHY HE IS WORRIED THAT IT COULD BECOME A PARADISE LOST

The year 2015 was indeed a battle that took its toll. The worry and all the financial troubles that have pursued him in this year have not yet released themselves from him. The rift with Marine Life has no closure at this time, but he is hoping that after the meeting he had with them not so long ago will be eventful. Yannis wants to move forward and he feels that he has come to a level in the 20 or so years he has been fighting for the conservation of the turtles on this island, he now needs help from other organizations to make the island's wildlife stay intact and be safe from any future developments from the tourism of the future.

Tourism plays a part in the demise of wildlife all around the world. This is something that we cannot stop, but we can control it simply by following the rules of conservation. The sanctuary that Yannis has built is of great importance to this island, and must be used for all injured wildlife and of course as an informational source for the flora and fauna as well.

The sanctuary could be used by schools that wish to teach their students about their island. Gerakas is truly a unique place, a Shangri-La that has everything that is good for wildlife. If you have never been there, then the understanding of this little part of the island would be unknown to you. I know that Yannis has a passion for this place and wishes to see it stay without contamination of buildings and overpopulation.

Sea Life, as I said before, had a meeting with Yannis and Jonna. They know themselves that the sanctuary is of great importance, so it is so important that the sanctuary does not become a white elephant and be allowed to fall into disrepair after all the hard work and money that has gone into the sanctuary. This would certainly be a crime. Zakynthos is a small island but of great importance to the world. Everyone that visits the sanctuary is impressed by how much one man has done. The efforts that Yannis has put in all these years do show their toll on him. I am not at all surprised in the least, anyone that has worked so hard for the love of his island deserves recognition. Everything that Yannis has done is about reaching his goal, this is why it is so vital that progress pursues the progress that has already been achieved.

The turtles on this island made up 80% of all turtles around the Med. This year (2015) has shown a decline. Some turtles have started to go to the mainland to nest as the island's beaches are becoming smaller due to tourism taking over the beaches, so the turtle, if we are not careful, will eventually be driven out completely. This is certainly not ideal; if we allow that to happen, then it will spell disaster for the turtle and indeed any other wildlife that relies on the beaches for all, or part of, their survival.

YANNIS VARDAKASTANIS' YOUNGER DAYS

These were certainly better times for the people of the island. Maybe not in a monetary sense, but the island was more virgin then and people, although did not have much, seemed to be happier. The island was an even more beautiful place than it is today. People had time for each other.

Yannis tells me how sad he is to see friends and families become separate from each other all because of money. This island is a paradise, but it is sad that some do not see it. They have become victims of the modern world and there seems to be no turning back. Of course, we all need to make a living, but for some it goes beyond that. They have forgotten what this island is all about.

'The good old days' – how many of us have said that? I know I have, even when I lived in London, the differences in the '50s when I was a boy were tremendous. Horse and carts carrying coal, beer from the local breweries, milkmen delivering the daily pint of milk, men employed to light the gas lights that stood in the streets in the evening, and then snub them out again in the morning with their poles with snub hoods on them, not unlike the ones that are used for candles.

This was a part of the 'good old days', which people of today do not understand. We had no money but everyone looked out for each other. If you had no food, then your neighbours would help, if you had no money, well you were on your own, nobody had any money, most things were bought on what we called 'tick', a sort of IOU.

This was how things were then, but for all its poverty, people would laugh and smile, go to the pub and have a knees-up with someone playing the piano, whether they could play well did not matter, it was the getting together that was important. Our next-door neighbour was a pub singer, she was awful, but entertaining, this is what was needed in those days. Television was only for the rich and we were told never to talk to them, as we classed them as snobs, someone that you avoided. Ridiculous really, it was only because they were much more fortunate than most. Those days, though, when there were more fields around and wildlife, those days just felt so much more relaxing than the manic lives we live today. More money; when you got more, then it was more that you wanted. This is a worldwide problem. So I know what Yannis means when he tells me the same thing about his island, and how much happier people, though very poor, were.

Dancing and singing were everyday occurrences, money never seem to matter too much. This is what life is really about and this is why Yannis is so passionate about the turtles and wildlife on this island. He would like to see many more of his fellow islanders have the same approach.

The difficulties that Yannis has come up against since he first started the sanctuary have been many, but I have never ever known one man to be so determined to keep the wildlife of Zakynthos healthy. This of course is what this very unique man is about. He is never worried about his own welfare, that he has proven time and time again. His marriage to his wife paid its toll, they went their separate ways. This is something that he did not want, but the future of his island was a more important factor. He has doubts on occasions, but I think that we all would.

His brothers, sisters, and parents did and still don't fully agree or understand his passions. They probably respect him though if nothing else. He understands their thoughts on him and although he would love to be close to them as he once was when he was just a young lad, he is stubborn in his thinking. These types of people that are willing to give up everything for the sake of conservation are true heroes in their own right. I have learnt a lot from Yannis; I don't always agree with him, but I respect what he is trying to do and he is never too shy to tell you his opinion. What I do know about him is that there are not too many people willing to give up as much as he has through these years.

He would love to see the people of the island become more concerned about the island that he loves so dearly. He told me not so long ago that the true Zakynthian came from the land, everyone took care of everything and everybody. This is still true for most, but alas there are a few that see no further than their bank accounts. Possessions have a great importance to them; greed has become an important factor in their lives and there seems to be no room for the survival of their island. Yannis hopes one day that these people will realise what is important in this world and change for the better. After all, what is better, having beauty surround them, or being engulfed in meaningless tinsel that could fall to the floor around them at any time? I know what I would prefer.

Yannis has told me that the last 25 years feels surreal. It seems only yesterday that when he was younger, he would sit around the table with his family, laughing, joking, everything was so simple. His family worked hard, as he did helping with the chores of life. He loved going for walks in the meadows and the woods that were near to where he lived, this he did without the luxury of shoes. This did not bother him; he loved the feel of the grasses beneath his feet and the rich soil that was so good to grow the produce that they needed to survive. Animals, birds even the insects, were fascinating to him. Flowers that grew in abundance would sway in the light breezes of summer. This was indeed a paradise, a paradise that he thought would never be endangered by the human race. This was going to be very true though; as the years ticked by, Yannis started to see the decay that was creeping rapidly into his island. He became a concerned person, watching as the glory of tourism developed at such a rate that it was making him dizzy!

Yes, he built a bar himself on the beach of Gerakas, as I have said much earlier in the book, but he realised that this was going to affect the wildlife and mostly the turtles. He could not accept that, so as I said before, he moved it away from the beach. This is where a lot of his troubles began. The troubles have continued even after all these years, but he was not to be deterred. The island, and all the other islands of Greece, have been affected by tourism. This is the way of the world now, but we must live in harmony with the nature on all the islands. It can be done! It's been done in America. Hotels are built very near the beach and many tourists visit, but the turtle survival rate is very healthy; it's because people care, so it is simple to achieve. This must be done everywhere in the world if we want to see the animals on this planet continue to live.

There is no going back from tourism, it is far too big and has come too far for a complete reversal. There is far too much money involved, people have to make a living, they cannot just stop. We must think, though, what makes a good part of the holiday that you have chosen; probably the countryside and the wildlife that comes with it. Pilot whales, for one, in Tenerife. Many people go out in boats to see these lovely creatures that cruise the seas. They don't, however, swamp them with surrounding boats that could stress them, the boats are limited, or at least were. The same with the turtles of Zakynthos; we must not smother them, we must give them the room so that they can swim around in safety and not be stressed by the overexcited tourist that are crammed on the turtle-spotting boats. The turtles that nest in Kalamaki and Lagana Bay are becoming fewer and fewer and they are starting to move further afield. This is something that we did not want, but it is happening now, so we must prevent any further demise and come up with an answer that will save these creatures from any more stress.

In the end it does not matter how much wealth we have. Surely the most important thing is your place of birth on this island. Anyone who was born on this island before tourism showed its head would surely prefer the old days, the old days that I once had when I was a child in London.

I refuse to except that the Zakynthians have abandoned their island just for the lust for money. Let's keep this island intact with all the beauty that surrounds us, and start to believe that we can all live together with the respect that we all deserve and that includes the wildlife as well. We live on a gemstone; this is why myself and my wife moved here. The island is unique, and the people also, but I sometimes wonder if we have not lost our way a little.

THE BOTTOM LINE

The year 2016 is going to be a very important time for the sanctuary. The sanctuary must start to accommodate the injured turtles and animals that fall foul, whether it is caused by the fishing nets and various other tools of the fishing industry. Whether it is caused by accidental or just injuries sustained by the turtles' predators. We all must take note of what Yannis Vardakastanis is trying to teach us.

Bobbie Fletcher, a reporter, made a programme about the turtles in 2001. Zakynthos was and still is the main island. Bobbie witnessed the helping of some of the turtles in that year, this included the three turtles that were sent to England. She witnessed a young turtle that was sent to Glyfada injured, then when it was well again, they transported the young turtle to Yannis' sanctuary for release at Gerakas.

It is these moments that will stick in your mind forever, knowing that the kindness of human beings has given this young turtle a new lease of life. It is a credit to these kind-hearted people that make conservation their life's work. We can all do a little for the wildlife no matter how small, it all helps. Put all the little pieces together, it becomes a jigsaw, and the big picture starts to come into view. This then makes a big difference to all wildlife that depend on how we react to saving it.

There is so much cruelty in the world caused for no other reason than money. We have to change; if not then the planet that we all live on and depend on will have no choice but to fall into a state of decay. A disaster, a disaster that will wipe out all life on the planet including us. We can do without plastic bags, palm oil and everything that is destroying this planet. Yannis Vardakastanis is just a small fish in a very large pond, but his efforts have had an impact in saving wildlife, but without help from other fish, big or small, everything that he has done to save wildlife will certainly one day become futile. This is when paradise will certainly be lost, and lost forever. Yannis Vardakastanis is a man that is deep in his beliefs, he will not faulter in his efforts for the saving of conservation. If nobody wants to help, so be it, in his mind, but he will never give up and if he has to, he will carry on, on his own. He knows he cannot do it all himself, but this man will give it a damn good try.

I am proud that I know this extraordinary man and what he believes in. Let's start to help him in his plight for the wildlife. The sanctuary always needs funds. Money is never easy to come by, we all know that, but just a little from all of us will complete the picture for the future of the turtles on this island. The cost of running the sanctuary runs into thousands. I know most of the money that Yannis makes with his bar goes into the sanctuary. It is hard to imagine how hard it is to get donations, even from other organisations, but what is money? Money is the root of all evil, but it is ironic that we need it to safeguard the wildlife on this planet. So it is very simple, do we want to live in a place that is heaven, or do we want to live in a *Paradise Lost*?

It has been my pleasure to write this book and about an ordinary man that has become so important to the island of Zakynthos.

Michael James Elves

The last three years have been very hard for Yannis. Earth Sea & Sky could no longer help Yannis financially and stopped their funding, which was a major blow to him. Yannis, though, is a fighter and does not know the word 'quit', so he will continue to fight for what he believes in, and will continue until he no longer can!

Yannis has a great passion for natural beauty on this island which he has known and been brought up with. Everything in nature he would love to preserve. He knows that the island has lost to tourism, but if he could just save a corner of it, then this would be brilliant. Yannis has started to collect farm machinery, relics from the '50s and early '60s. He has an old beautiful tractor and a combine harvester, which he intends using on the land that he is hoping to purchase. This would certainly help the wildlife as it would make food for the wildlife more accessible.

BAD NEWS FOR THE TURTLES

This year (2019) has certainly not been good for the turtles. Some of the turtles that have lived around the island of Zakynthos for years have been killed or badly injured solely from so called turtle-spotting boats. One turtle was cut to pieces as the blades of a boat ran straight over it. This horrified onlookers from another boat as they could see blood gushing out of the poor creature. Needless to say, it was killed. Some of the boats are far too big to be there, but of course their sole purpose is money. The speed limit is six knots an hour, but clearly by the wake that the boat is making, it is far greater, this more so in the bay of Kalamaki. This needs to be stopped so that no further senseless injuries and deaths occur.

LOCAL INVOLVEMENT

The sanctuary has had many volunteers throughout the years. People from all over the world have come over and supported the sanctuary; England, America and as far away as New Zealand, but now Yannis wants to get the local people of Zakynthos and people from other countries that have chosen to live here to help him win the battle, people that want to see this island stay in its natural state. I hope that this will happen for him.

The state of the world today is very disturbing, this must change or our world will be the one that pays a heavy price.

There is hope for this island and the planet and maybe we will see the light at the end of the tunnel.

We can change things, it's just a matter of wanting to!

TURTLE NESTS

I would like to remind you of some simple rules of the beach where turtles lay their eggs.

Please do not go near the nests, they are mostly recognised by the frameworks that are put over the top of a nesting to protect them. If you go near them, then it is possible that the pressure from your feet will harden the sand and make it difficult for the hatchlings.

Vibrations from your feet can also make them hatch too soon.

Stay well away from the area when playing such games as football.

There is a good possibility that there are nests that have not been discovered, so once again it is vital that you stay well away.

Sunbeds and parasols can play a tragic part in the hatchlings demise, keep to the water's edge as much as possible where the sand is damper. Turtles won't lay their eggs in damp sand; it would be much harder for them to dig and also the eggs would drown.

When making sandcastles and digging holes in the sand, make sure that at the end of the day the sandcastles are knocked down and the sand made flat. Fill in all holes, they might be only small holes, but to a new hatchling trying to get to the water's edge, it certainly could become life or death for them. They have enough enemies already, we do not wish to make it any harder for them.

RUBBISH REMINDER

When leaving the beach please ensure that you have not left any rubbish behind such as plastic bags, plastic cups and bottles, straws, etc.; all these items can kill a turtle and give them a horrific death!

The rule is leave the beach tiday and take all rubbish with you.

The preservation of this island is paramount. We all know that there are natural hazards that can destroy the environment. For example, there are a couple of beaches that have natural clay. Small cliff-like areas where it is said that if you cover yourself with this clay it will exfoliate you (taking dead skin off one's body). Natural clay is known to absorb impurities, so it is well known that there are a lot of people covering themselves with this clay and then later washing it off in the sea. It's a splendid feeling and your body feels fresh and alive.

The beach of Gerakas and also Porto Azorro have this clay, but the downside is in the beaches' struggle to survive the natural corrosion. What we do not realise is that every time that we take a handful of clay to smother ourselves with, we are in fact accelerating the demise of the beaches. This would be devastating for everybody, so you can see that it is a real life problem. I certainly do not want to be tarred with the name killjoy, but if everybody stopped indulging themselves with the clay it would certainly delay the corrosion for a lot longer.

Shells and stones have their part to play on the beaches as well. There is nothing nicer than to amble along the beach picking up shells and some multi-coloured stones. I have done this myself, then one day I stopped and thought about it. If everybody took shells and stones away from the beaches, this also in turn would accelerate their demise! People will never stop doing these things, but imagine if everybody was to take a bag full of shells, as I said just now, we have all done it, somewhere along the line there will be much less of a beach. Maybe just take one or two; this I know could cause the same problem, but in a much less accelerated form. Think about it, you would be doing the beaches a favour, not just the beaches of Zakynthos, but every beach in the world.

I know reading this makes me sound like a real misery, but the truth of it all is that it is true. After all, it's only us that is destroying the world and basically it is only us that can change it. In years ahead, definitely after I have left this world, there will be no beaches, no wildlife and nothing for the people of the future. It's a bleak thought, let's not let it happen.

Yannis said to me the other day, "How many millions of people have gone on to the beaches throughout the years and left with sand on their clothing and shoes."

I thought it daft at first, then I thought, *you know what, he is right*. How many tonnes of sand have been taken off the beaches never to return! I hope that anyone who purchases this book will think a totally different way after reading.

Let's keep this beautiful world of ours healthy!

MICHAEL JAMES ELVES.

A SNAKE SUNBATHING ON ALYKES BEACH.

A KINGFISHER TAKING A WELL-EARNED BREAK AFTER
FISHING ON THE STREAM IN ALYKES NEAR THE BEACH.

HERE ARE SOME EXAMPLES OF PLANTATION THAT WILL
BE SEEN ON THE SALT LAKES OF ALYKES, BUT THERE IS AN
ARRAY OF PLANT LIFE ALL AROUND IN DIFFERENT COLOURS.

THIS, I'M SAD TO SAY, IS ALSO ON THE SALT LAKES, AND IT IS ONLY TOO
COMMON. PLASTIC BOTTLES STREWN ALL OVER THE PLACE RATHER THAN
TAKE THE TIME AND ENERGY TO PUT IT IN ITS RIGHTFUL PLACE.

A VIEW OF GERAKAS BEACH IN MAY.

ANOTHER VIEW OF GERAKAS BEACH, THIS TIME WITH TURTLE
NESTS, WHICH ARE MADE VISUAL BY THE WOODEN FRAMES.

THE SALT LAKES OF ALYKES HOLDS A NUMBER OF BIRDS. ABOVE YOU WILL
SEE THE EGRET AND IBIS, BOTH WADING BIRDS. THE IBIS IS NOT AS
COMMON ON THE LAKES, SO IT IS NICE TO SEE THEM. THESE BIRDS COME
FROM THE THRESKIORNITHIDAE FAMILY AND ARE BLACK WITH A LONG
CURVED BEAK. BELOW IS A NICE SHOT OF SOME OF THE SLAT LAKES. ON THE
SMALL ISLAND THERE IS A HERON GETTING READY TO GO FISHING.

SOME OF THE INSECTS THAT CAN BE FOUND ON THE ISLAND. ABOVE IS A
BEAUTIFUL PREYING MANTIS. THIS, IN FACT, RESIDES IN OUR GARDEN IN
ONE OF THE FLOWER POTS, AND BELOW A RATHER LARGE GREEN BEETLE.
THIS WAS ALSO IN OUR GARDEN, RESTING ON THE WALL OF THE HOUSE.

A WORKING BEE BUSILY COLLECTING POLLEN FROM THIS RATHER SPLENDID
PLANT. BEES ARE SO VERY IMPORTANT TO THE PLANET.

BELOW WE HAVE SOME CATERPILLARS FEEDING ON A SEA DAFFODIL.
I'M NOT SURE WHAT TYPE THESE CATERPILLARS ARE, THOUGH.

THIS AWFUL SIGHT WAS WASHED UP ON KALAMAKI BEACH AND
LEFT THERE FOR A PERIOD OF NINE DAYS BEFORE IT WAS MOVED TO A SAFER
PLACE. AS YOU CAN SEE, THE LABEL ON THE DRUM SUGGESTS THAT IT IS
HARMFUL. THE CONTENTS IN THAT TIME HAD SPILLED ONTO THE SANDS, AND
NO DOUBT INTO THE SEA. THE DRUM WAS MOVED TO A SAFER PLACE NEAR
THE DUNES ON CRYSTAL BEACH, BY MYSELF!

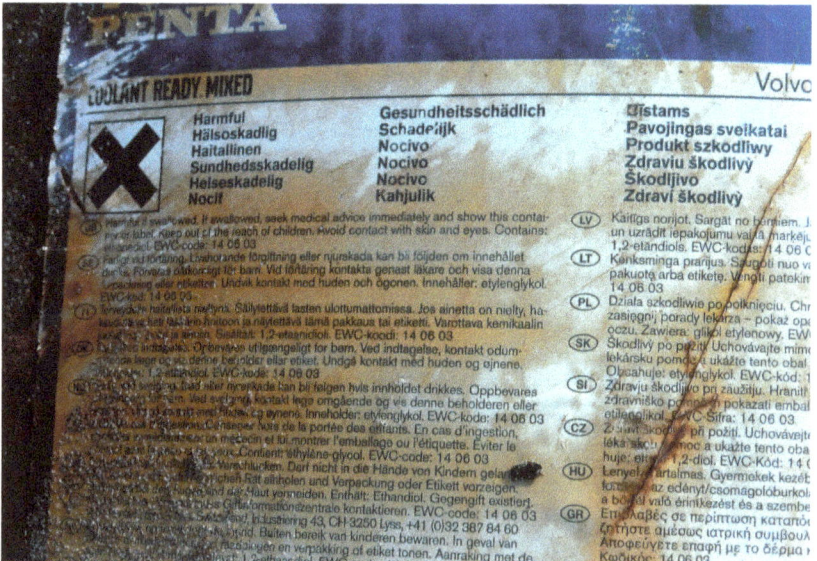

A VISITOR FROM AMERICA, TOMMY CUTT, CHIEF CONSERVATION
OFFICER FOR THE LOGGERHEAD MARINE LIFE CENTRE, SPENT TWO WEEKS AT
THE SANCTUARY. HE WAS VERY IMPRESSED WITH WHAT YANNIS HAS
ACHIEVED. FROM LEFT TO RIGHT: MAUREEN, MY WIFE; EMILY, ASSISTANT
PROJECT MANAGER; TOMMY CUTT; JONNA PEDERSEN, PROJECT MANAGER;
YANNIS VARDAKASTANIS, DIRECTOR; AND LAST BUT HOPEFULLY NOT LEAST,
MYSELF, MICHAEL JAMES ELVES.

SOME OF THE WILD FLOWERS OPPOSITE THE SANCTUARY IN EARLY SUMMER.

A BEAUTIFUL VIEW OF THE MEADOWS OPPOSITE THE TURTLE SANCTUARY.

BELOW, ANOTHER COLOURFUL SCENE OF THE COASTAL PATH ABOVE GERAKAS BEACH, WHICH TAKES YOU TO A FASCINATING AREA WHICH LOOKS A BIT LIKE THE MOON'S SURFACE. INCREDIBLE.

THE SEA TURTLE RESCUE CENTRE

THE LEGENDARY STRENGTH OF THE SEA TURTLE IS CENTRAL
TO THE CREATION MYTHOLOGY OF MANY PEOPLE, WHO BELIEVED THAT IF
THE SEA TURTLE DISAPPEARED, THE WORLD WOULD END.
THIS ANCIENT MAYAN SYMBOL DEPICTS THE SEA TURTLE SWIMMING IN THE
WORLD'S INFINITE SEA TO ETERNALLY SEPARATE EARTH FROM SKY. BELOW,
GERAKAS BEACH. THE MAYAN SYMBOL IS SEEN AT THE TOP OF THE
WELCOME TO GERAKAS BOARD.

ABOVE A VIEW FROM KALAMAKI BEACH
OVERLOOKING KERI, AND BELOW A VIEW FROM
KALAMAKI LOOKING OVER TOWARDS GERAKAS.

STANDING ON TOP OF THE HILL ABOVE DAFNI
BEACH, THERE IS THIS SUPERB VIEW ACROSS THE
SEA, WITH PELOUZO ISLAND TO YOUR LEFT.

BELOW, A VIEW FROM THE BEACH OF GERAKAS
BEFORE THE TURTLES HAVE NESTED.

THE WOODCHAT SHRIKE SEEN HERE TAKING A REST, AND
TAKING IN THE BEAUTIFUL VIEW ACROSS THE KERI LAKE.

BELOW, A GREEN LIZARD WELL CAMOUFLAGED
IN THE UNDERGROWTH.

THE VERY LARGE TURTLE THAT SITS PROUDLY AT THE ENTRANCE OF THE
TURTLE SANCTUARY, WHOSE NAME IS ZANTOS, WAS ALL BLUE, BUT IT WAS
DECIDED BY YANNIS AND JONNA THAT HE NEEDED A FACELIFT.

I WAS GIVEN THE PRIVILEGE TO PAINT ZANTOS
WITH MORE NOTICEABLE COLOURS.

ABOVE, I AM JUST PUTTING THE FINISHING TOUCHES TO
ZANTOS, THE FACELIFT TOOK ABOUT 50 HOURS. BELOW IS
THE COMPLETED ZANTOS, AND HOPEFULLY HE LOOKS MORE HANDSOME
AND EVEN MORE PROUD THAN BEFORE.

THIS PICTURE OF A GRASSHOPPER WAS TAKEN BY MY WIFE, MAUREEN,
IN OUR GARDEN. WHAT A BEAUTIFUL CREATURE.
BELOW IS ANOTHER PICTURE OF A TERRAPIN THAT LIVES IN
THE FRESHWATER STREAMS OF KERI. IT IS SUCH A WORTHY
PICTURE I FELT IT NEEDED TO BE IN THE BOOK.

THESE PICTURES OF RUBBISH WERE TAKEN IN ABOUT 2002 AND
I AM SADDENED TO SAY THAT THE PROBLEM IS STILL WITH US!

WE ARE GUARDING THIS PLACE FOR THOSE WHO HAVE NOT YET BEEN BORN.

A personal view by Yannis Vardakastanis, an Ionian islander

When I was a child there were long hot summer days when it was just me and the turtles. Long before my island home became a package tourist destination. I can remember walking barefoot down through the woods and across the meadows and olive groves that led to Gerakas and the big blue. The buzz of insects, the singing of the birds and the sound of the sea was music to my ears. I didn't fully appreciate it at the time, but I was living in God's pocket. It was the only world I knew and I probably thought every other kid in the world was enjoying life in a similar landscape.

We did not have very much in those days. We were very poor in fact, but as I have grown older and visited a good number of the many countries of this world, I have come to realise that less is more, that living at one with nature is the true home of the human spirit and being born into it was my great fortune.

The summer days are still as long and hot as they were when I was a child, but I rarely find myself alone with the turtles on the Gerakas beach of today. When I do, I whisper my apologies and promise them help is coming.

MAYBE WE CANNOT SAVE THE WORLD, BUT WITH YOUR SUPPORT WE CAN SAVE A LITTLE CORNER OF IT.

EARTH, SEA & SKY

AUTHOR'S SUMMARY

I hope that this book will convince people that the planet that we live on is the only one that we have. You must decide for yourselves whether you would like to preserve it for the future of the human race and the wildlife that exists with us. We need to change our views to keep this planet healthy. If not, then we can only blame ourselves for the planet's certain decline. It is us that is destroying everything that we need to survive purely and mostly for money.

If we wish the human race to survive, then we must act now and change for a better world for our children's sake and for the wildlife that depends on us for their existence.

AUTHOR'S NOTE

SOME OF THE THINGS THAT ARE MENTIONED IN THE BOOK HAVE BEEN PASSED ON TO ME, AND I HAVE BEEN ASSURED THAT THEY ARE CORRECT AT THE TIME OF WRITING.

MICHAEL JAMES ELVES

EPILOGUE

More than 30 years have passed since Yannis Vardakastanis started the centre striving to save the turtles that come to the island of Zakynthos. This has been a non-stop battle for him and it is starting to take its toll. He has become exhausted and ill health has started to show its ugly head. Yannis realises that he will not be able to continue his work for much longer.

Family feuds have been a common issue also which has affected him badly in the work for preservation, as money has had a big impact towards his family and is causing unrest between them, which involves Yannis and is making it more impossible for him to carry on.

Tourism has, in the last 30 years, become a big problem and the beaches are starting to decay. The amount of stones that are taking over the beach of Gerakas also is showing a grim future for the loggerhead turtle and of course the sunbeds that now have to be set up further along the beach because of the stones. Well, that is also a concern as they are taking more of the sandy part of the beach which lessens the area for the turtles to nest.

Maybe not now, but a few years into the future, the beach of Gerakas will not be able to play its part for the turtles that lay their eggs there, leaving it barren for the loggerhead.

Yannis knows this and realises that he is fighting a losing battle. His love for the turtles is unparalleled and it saddens him to see a possible end to these creatures that grace the island year after year.

It is a devastating thought that he is starting to feel defeated. I have known Yannis for a number of years and I can see the spark that he once had in his eyes starting to die, but for his own sake he must start to think about himself before he becomes more unwell and for this, he must start to think of a graceful retirement.

I have never known a man so devoted in his love for the turtles and the island of Zakynthos, which he has lived on since he was a very young boy.

This man, though, is very hard to predict, so it would never surprise me to see him carry on his work but as a friend I would like to see him (for his own good) bow out and retire gracefully. Go somewhere remote where he can live a life without any of the modern-day madness that most of us live in, where he can once again become part of nature that he so dearly loves.

Yannis Vardakastanis has done so much more than most in the last 30 years or more. His dedication to the wildlife that surrounds us is an inspiration to us all. If we did but a fraction of what this extraordinary man has done, we would be proud of ourselves and also the world would be a much more stable place for the future of nature and to mankind itself.

So we must all help to keep our planet healthy. It doesn't take much; if we all do a little then this will become massive, or if not, let's just sit around and let someone else do it, but then we must prepare ourselves for the worst.

A PARADISE LOST!

UPDATE 2022

Gerakas beach, this year, seems to have a problem with crabs. These crabs have become many and have never been spotted before on the beach of Gerakas. The crabs are apparently entering the nests of the turtles and destroying the whole nest, which may hold as many as 180 eggs! This would become a huge problem. The crabs are a predator of the young hatchlings that try to make it to the sea, so if they are entering the nests, which we have seen first-hand, then this could be devastating!

These crabs make burrows in the sand, waiting for some unfortunate hatchling to go past, then they grab them and pull the hatchling into its tomb where it will have a gory end.

In England, in Cornwall, there is an influx of spider crabs, which has never been known before! This, I believe, is due to global warming. The world is changing! The crabs in Gerakas, though, are ghost crabs (raiders of the night). Males are larger than the females and they live up to three years. These crabs have four pairs of legs and one pair of white claws. Their eyestalks can move 360 degrees, their egg masses have an average of between two and eight million eggs. The crabs burrow about four feet into the sand where they also hibernate.

The lionfish is becoming a problem also in and around Greece, as they have increased threefold in the last two years. These fish have eighteen stingers, which can harm humans. The sting is very painful and could be dangerous.

In England they have another problem, and that problem is sharks. They are becoming more evident. This, once again, is due to global warming and the sharks are coming into more shallow waters for the fish. The water around the UK is becoming warmer and, of course, it will become a problem, I think, in the near future. There is nothing we can do about this; the world is changing and so are the creatures that live here!

TURTLES IN CALIFORNIA

For the last four years there has only been female from the nests. This is because of climate change. If the sand's temperature is higher than 88.8 Fahrenheit, then this will occur. If the sand is much cooler, then the likelihood will be all males. Normally the males occur when the nest hole is deeper. However, if the nest depth is in between the hotter and cooler sand, then the outcome would be of both sexes. Having fewer males, though, could lead to unsustainable poor genetic diversity among the sea turtles. This could be a growing concern for the future.

www.ingramcontent.com/pod-product-compliance
Lightning Source LLC
Chambersburg PA
CBHW041930260326
41914CB00009B/1244